S U P
THE
OF THE
FORTRESS
OF SOLITUDE
SUPERMAN created by
JERRY SIEGEL and JOE SHUSTER

# SUPERMAN

**"MUSCLES FOR SALE"**
*(From SUPERMAN #17, 1942)*
Writer: JERRY SIEGEL
Artist: JOHN SIKELA

**"THE SUPER-KEY TO FORT SUPERMAN"**
*(From ACTION COMICS #241, 1958)*
Writer: JERRY COLEMAN
Penciller: WAYNE BORING
Inker: STAN KAYE
Cover: CURT SWAN & STAN KAYE

**"SUPERMAN'S FORTRESSES OF SOLITUDE"**
*(From ACTION COMICS #261, 1960)*
Writer: JERRY SIEGEL
Penciller: WAYNE BORING
Inker: STAN KAYE
Cover: CURT SWAN & STAN KAYE

**"FORTRESS OF FEAR"**
*(From DC SPECIAL SERIES #26, 1981)*
Writer: ROY THOMAS
Penciller: ROSS ANDRU
Inker: ROMEO TANGHAL
Cover: ROSS ANDRU & DICK GIORDANO

**"MEMORIES OF KRYPTON'S PAST"**
*(From ACTION COMICS ANNUAL #2, 1989)*
Writers: JERRY ORDWAY, GEORGE PÉREZ, ROGER STERN
Pencillers: JERRY ORDWAY, MIKE MIGNOLA, CURT SWAN
Inkers: JOHN STATEMA, GEORGE PÉREZ, BRETT BREEDING
Cover: GEORGE PÉREZ & JERRY ORDWAY

**"CREATION STORY"**
*(From SUPERMAN: THE MAN OF STEEL #100, 2000)*
Writer: MARK SCHULTZ
Penciller: DOUG MAHNKE
Inker: TOM NGUYEN
Cover: DOUG MAHNKE & TOM NGUYEN

**"SECRETS OF THE FORTRESS OF SOLITUDE"**
*(From ACTION COMICS ANNUAL #10, 2007)*
Writers: GEOFF JOHNS, RICHARD DONNER
Penciller: PHIL JIMENEZ
Inker: ANDY LANNING

***Mort Weisinger*** *Len Wein* ***Mike Carlin*** ***Eddie Berganza*** ***Matt Idelson*** *Editors – Original Series*
***Mike W. Barr*** ***Maureen McTigue*** ***Nachie Castro*** *Associate Editors – Original Series* | ***Renée Witterstaetter*** *Assistant Editor – Original Series*
***Robin Wildman*** *Editor* | ***Robbin Brosterman*** *Design Director - Books* | ***Curtis King Jr.*** *Publication Design*

***Eddie Berganza*** *Executive Editor* | ***Bob Harras*** *Editor-in-Chief*

***Diane Nelson*** *President* | ***Dan DiDio*** *and* ***Jim Lee*** *Co-Publishers* | ***Geoff Johns*** *Chief Creative Officer*
***John Rood*** *Executive VP – Sales, Marketing and Business Development* | ***Amy Genkins*** *Senior VP – Business and Legal Affairs*
***Nairi Gardiner*** *Senior VP – Finance* | ***Jeff Boison*** *VP – Publishing Operations* | ***Mark Chiarello*** *VP – Art Direction and Design*
***John Cunningham*** *VP – Marketing* | ***Terri Cunningham*** *VP – Talent Relations and Services*
***Alison Gill*** *Senior VP – Manufacturing and Operations* | ***David Hyde*** *VP – Publicity* | ***Hank Kanalz*** *Senior VP – Digital*
***Jay Kogan*** *VP – Business and Legal Affairs, Publishing* | ***Jack Mahan*** *VP – Business Affairs, Talent*
***Nick Napolitano*** *VP – Manufacturing Administration* | ***Sue Pohja*** *VP – Book Sales* | ***Courtney Simmons*** *Senior VP – Publicity*
***Bob Wayne*** *Senior VP – Sales*

**SUPERMAN: THE SECRETS OF THE FORTRESS OF SOLITUDE**


*DC COMICS 1700 Broadway, New York, NY 10019*
*A Warner Bros. Entertainment Company*
*Printed by RR Donnelley, Willard, OH, USA. 3/23/12. First Printing.*
*ISBN: 978-1-4012-3423-2*

SUPERMAN
REG. U.S. PAT. OFF.
by JERRY SIEGEL and JOE SHUSTER
I'D LIKE TO ENROLL, SIR, AND BECOME STRONG-- LIKE YOU!
WHA--?
"STEP RIGHT UP, FOLKS! COME ONE, COME ALL! YOU, TOO, CAN BE A MIGHTY MAN, A MUSCULAR MARVEL, THE DELIGHT OF THE DAMSELS, A SAMPSON OF STRENGTH!"---YOU'VE SEEN DOZENS OF ADS SUCH AS THESE BECAUSE BODY BUILDING NOWADAYS IS BIG BUSINESS. SMALL WONDER, THEN, THAT LOIS LANE INSISTED CLARK KENT ENROLL IN A MUSCLE-BUILDING CLASS-- FOR THE GIRL-REPORTER HAD NO WAY OF KNOWING THAT THE APPARENTLY MEEK, COWARDLY DAILY PLANET SCRIBE IS IN REALITY SUPERMAN, THE WORLD'S MOST POWERFUL MAN! WHAT AT FIRST PROMISES TO BE THE LAUGH OF THE CENTURY TURNS INTO DYNAMIC DRAMA AS THE MIGHTY MAN OF TOMORROW FLASHES THRU THE COMPLEX MYSTERY THAT SHROUDS THE CHUCKLE-PRODUCING YET THRILL-PROVOKING ADVENTURE OF.... "MUSCLES FOR SALE!"
1

TO ONE OF METROPOLIS' MOST
XCLUSIVE JEWELRY ESTABLISH-
ENTS HESITANTLY ENTERS A
EEK INDIVIDUAL....
WHAT CAN I DO
FOR YOU, SIR?
ER... I...
I'M JUST
LOOKING
AROUND.

SO HELP ME, BUT DOESN'T THAT LITTLE SQUIRT LOOK LIKE A COMIC ARTIST'S CONCEPTION OF MR. NOBODY?
HE LOOKS AS THOUGH HE HASN'T MORE THAN A FEW DOLLARS IN THIS WORLD. WATCH ME HAVE SOME FUN WITH HIM!
WOULD YOU BE INTERESTED IN THIS LITTLE TRINKET-- PRICE A MERE $75,000?
I--I MIGHT BE INTERESTED, AT THAT!

IN FACT, I'LL TAKE IT WITH ME RIGHT NOW!
A HOLDUP!

IMMEDIATELY, THE STORE DETECTIVE GOES INTO ACTION...
TRYING TO PLAY TOUGH, EH? WHY, YOU LITTLE HALF-PINT SQUIRT, I'LL...!
I WARN YOU! KEEP AWAY OR I'LL BE FORCED TO RESORT TO PHYSICAL VIOLENCE, SOMETHING WHICH I ORDINARILY ABHOR!

OWWW-WWW!
I WARNED YOU NOT TO TANGLE WITH SOMEONE OF MY SUPERIOR STATURE!
2

A THIEF! CLARK! STOP HIM!
YOU MEAN-- SINGLE-HANDED? ("-POLICE APPROACHING! THEY'LL HANDLE HIM!-")
JEWELRY STORE

STOP, I SAY! ("-GOT TO KEEP IN CHARACTER!-")
ONE SIDE! I'M A HUMAN CANNON BALL!
ST

DELIBERATELY, CLARK PERMITS HIMSELF TO BE THRUST ASIDE.
LIKE A BREEZE!
OO-OOF! ("-NOW IT'S UP TO THE POLICE!-")
YOU CLUMSY FOOL! YO LET HIM G PAST YOU

HUH? A BLOOMIN' KANGAROO!
IT'S NOT AS DIFFICULT AS IT LOOKS!

EXCUSE ME, LOIS! ("-HE ELUDED THE POLICE! NOW TO GET AFTER HIM AS SUPERMAN!-")
TRYING TO SLIP AWAY A PHONE IN T STORY, EH? YOU DON'T! STICKING W YOU!

BUT AFTER THEY REPORT THE OCCURRENCE TO THE DAILY PLANET...
(PUFF! PUFF!) WAIT FOR ME! I CAN HARDLY KEEP UP WITH YOU!
WHAT A MISERABLE SPECIMEN OF HUMANITY YOU ARE! FRANKLY, I'M ASHAMED TO BE SEEN WITH YOU!
DRUG
3

LATER-- IN THE SUBWAY
BUT, LOIS-YOU CAN'T EXPECT EVERYONE TO BE A SUPERMAN!
DON'T SPEAK TO ME!

A CONSPICUOUS ADVERTI-MENT CATCHES LOIS' STARTLED INTEREST
WELL!!

ADVERTISEMENT
WOULD YOU LIKE TO HAVE MUSCLES?
I'VE BUILT HUNDREDS OF SUPER BODIES. I CAN DO THE SAME FOR YOU!
MIKE MOSBY'S
USCLE-ORIUM

WHY DON'T YOU GO TO MOSBY'S GYM, CLARK, AND MOLD YOUR FLABBY MUSCLES INTO SINEWS OF STEEL?
BUT THAT WOULD REQUIRE EXERCISE!
SUBWAY

I MIGHT HAVE EXPECTED A REMARK LIKE THAT FROM YOU! YOU'RE SO SPINELESS SOMEONE OUGHT TO DONATE YOU TO THE MUSEUM OF NATURAL HISTORY!
BUT---!
BUS STOP

STEPPING INTO AN ALLEY, CLARK SHEDS HIS OUTER GARMENTS...
I THOUGHT I COULDN'T SINK ANY LOWER IN LOIS' ESTIMATION, BUT IT LOOKS AS THO I'VE ACHIEVED THE IMPOSSIBLE!

AND A MOMENT LATER IS TRANSFORMED O THE WORLD'S MOST POWERFUL CRIME-IGHTER... SUPERMAN!
THERE'S A LITTLE JOB I'VE STILL TO FINISH!
4

UP-UP AND AWAY!!

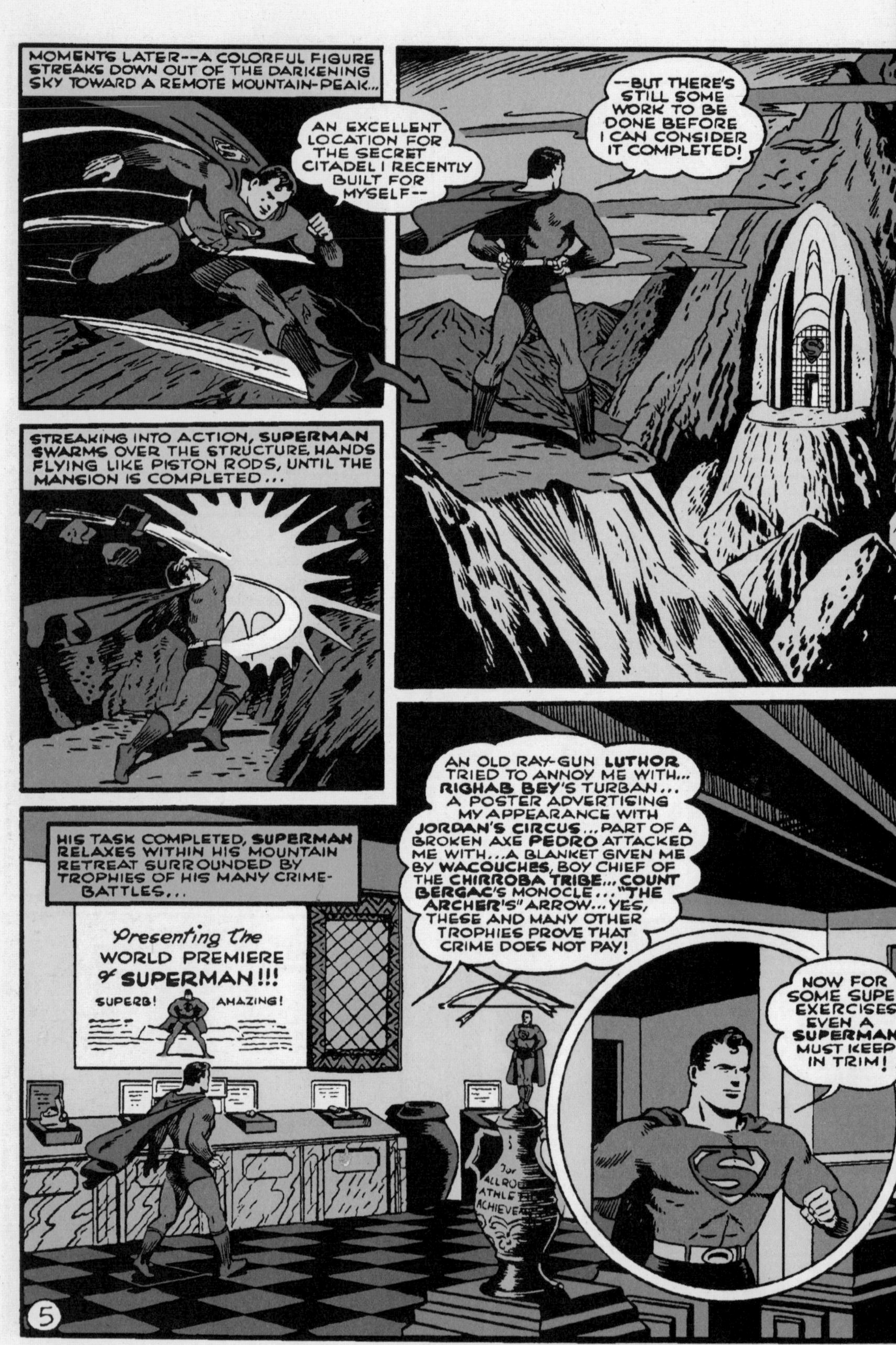
MOMENTS LATER--A COLORFUL FIGURE STREAKS DOWN OUT OF THE DARKENING SKY TOWARD A REMOTE MOUNTAIN-PEAK...
AN EXCELLENT LOCATION FOR THE SECRET CITADEL I RECENTLY BUILT FOR MYSELF--
--BUT THERE'S STILL SOME WORK TO BE DONE BEFORE I CAN CONSIDER IT COMPLETED!
STREAKING INTO ACTION, SUPERMAN SWARMS OVER THE STRUCTURE, HANDS FLYING LIKE PISTON RODS, UNTIL THE MANSION IS COMPLETED...
HIS TASK COMPLETED, SUPERMAN RELAXES WITHIN HIS MOUNTAIN RETREAT SURROUNDED BY TROPHIES OF HIS MANY CRIME-BATTLES...
Presenting the WORLD PREMIERE of SUPERMAN!!!
SUPERB! AMAZING!
AN OLD RAY-GUN LUTHOR TRIED TO ANNOY ME WITH... RIGHAB BEY'S TURBAN... A POSTER ADVERTISING MY APPEARANCE WITH JORDAN'S CIRCUS... PART OF A BROKEN AXE PEDRO ATTACKED ME WITH... A BLANKET GIVEN ME BY WACOUCHES, BOY CHIEF OF THE CHIRROBA TRIBE... COUNT BERGAC'S MONOCLE... "THE ARCHER'S" ARROW... YES, THESE AND MANY OTHER TROPHIES PROVE THAT CRIME DOES NOT PAY!
NOW FOR SOME SUPE EXERCISES EVEN A SUPERMAN MUST KEEP IN TRIM!
5

SUPERMAN INDULGES IN ACROBATICS THAT WOULD CAUSE ANY GYM ENTHUSIAST TO DOUBT HIS EYESIGHT. HE SPEEDS UP AND DOWN A LONG ROPE-- BACKWARDS!
THIS OUGHT TO BE A POPULAR SPORT IN CHINA!
NOT CONTENT WITH CHINNING IN THE CONVENTIONAL MANNER, HE RAISES AND LOWERS THE HUGE BAR TO HIS CHIN...!
DOIN' IT THE HARD WAY!
'ROUND AND 'ROUND THE CIRCULAR TRACK HE RACES AT SO GREAT A SPEED THERE APPEARS TO BE ONE CONTINUOUS BODY GIRDLING THE TRACK!
AT THIS RATE, I'LL CATCH UP WITH MYSELF!!
GOOD FOR THE SHOULDER-BLADES!
ROBBERY IN PROGRESS AT MINTON MUSEUM!
BUSINESS BEFORE PLEASURE!
AS SUPERMAN SPRINGS INTO THE AIR TO PERFORM ANOTHER STUNT, HIS SUPER-SENSITIVE HEARING PICKS UP A POLICE SHORT-WAVE BROADCAST THAT CAUSES HIM TO CHANGE THE DIRECTION OF HIS LEAP...

AT THE MINTON MUSEUM, A ROTUND BANDIT HOLDS THE GUARDS AT BAY AS HE ANNEXES AN EXHIBIT OF VALUABLE GEMS...
YOU WON'T GET AWAY WITH THIS!
STRANGELY ENOUGH, I'M SUPREMELY CONFIDENT THAT I WILL!
THEN HERE'S WHERE YOU GET A RUDE SHOCK!
SUPERMAN
YOU CAN PUT THOSE GEMS RIGHT BACK WHERE YOU GOT THEM!
I'M NOT READY TO GIVE UP-- YET!
DELIBERATELY, THE CORPULENT CRIMINAL FIRES A BARRAGE OF BULLETS AT THE CHANDELIER OVERHEAD. SEVERED FROM ITS BASE, IT TOPPLES DOWN TOWARD THE STARTLED GUARDS BELOW...
THAT OUGHT TO KEEP YOU BUSY!
BUT NOT FOR LONG
IT WILL BE LONG ENOUGH FOR ME TO ESCAPE!
MEANWHILE--CRASHING HEAD-ON INTO THE FALLING CHANDELIER, SUPERMAN BATTERS IT ASIDE...
MOVE OVER!
...SO THAT IT MISSES IT
INTENDED VICTIMS!
WE OWE YOU OUR LIVES!
NEXT ON THE PROGRAM--I'VE GOT TO PREVENT FAT BOY'S ESCA
7

ALIGHTING, **SUPERMAN** TURNS HIS CAPTIVE OVER TO POLICE WHO HAVE JUST REACHED THE SCENE...

SUPERMAN! KNOW ANYTHING ABOUT THE ROBBERY GOING ON IN THE MUSEUM?

JUST ENOUGH TO LEAVE THE CULPRIT IN YOUR HANDS!

THERE HAVE BEEN A NUMBER OF BOLD CRIMES LATELY, PULLED BY UNGAINLY MEN WHO LOOK ANYTHING BUT FORMIDABLE. THE LATEST ATTEMPT WAS FOILED AT THE **MINTON MUSEUM** LAST NIGHT BY **SUPERMAN**. I WANT BOTH OF YOU TO VISIT THE JAIL AND LEARN WHAT YOU CAN.

LET'S GO, CLARK. THAT IS, IF YOU CAN SUMMON UP ENOUGH ENERGY!

BE RIGHT WITH YOU! AND NEVER MIND THE CRACKS!

LATER--
WHAT I CAN'T UNDERSTAND, MR. BRANT, IS WHY A QUIET, SANE, RESPECTABLE BUSINESS MAN OF YOUR FINE INTEGRITY SHOULD HAVE TURNED TO CRIME.
DON'T PREACH TO ME!
GEORGE-- GEORGE... THAT DOESN'T SOUND LIKE YOU AT ALL!

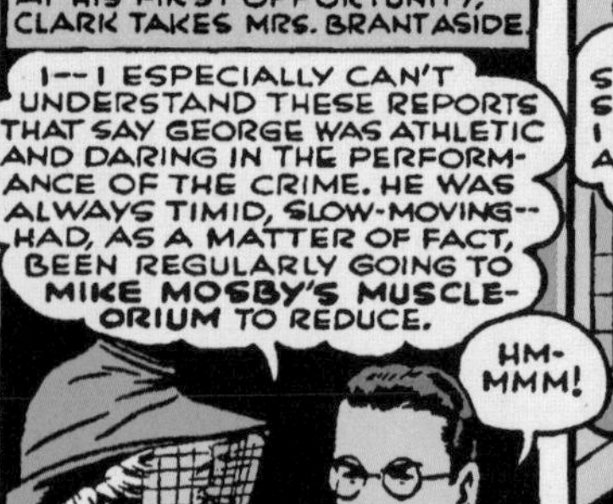
AT HIS FIRST OPPORTUNITY, CLARK TAKES MRS. BRANT ASIDE.
I-- I ESPECIALLY CAN'T UNDERSTAND THESE REPORTS THAT SAY GEORGE WAS ATHLETIC AND DARING IN THE PERFORMANCE OF THE CRIME. HE WAS ALWAYS TIMID, SLOW-MOVING-- HAD, AS A MATTER OF FACT, BEEN REGULARLY GOING TO MIKE MOSBY'S MUSCLE-ORIUM TO REDUCE.
HM-MMM!

LOIS... I'VE BEEN GIVING YOUR SUGGESTION SOME SERIOUS THOUGHT. I THINK I'LL ENROLL AT MOSBY'S GYM AFTER ALL!

MR. MOSBY, CLARK IS PUNY AND WEAK-- EVERYONE ALWAYS PICKS ON HIM...
("-HERE'S WHERE I MAKE A BIG IMPRESSION ON THIS SWELL DISH BY BEATING UP HER BOY FRIEND!-") GET INTO A GYM SUIT, KENT. WE'LL GIVE MISS LANE A PREVIEW OF THE TOUGHENING PROCESS YOU'LL RECEIVE HERE!
ULP! ("-THAT LITTLE FELLOW STROLLING BY! HE'S THE CHAP WHO ROBBED THE JEWELRY STORE!-")

NOT BAD! WHY, CLARK-- YOU HAVEN'T SUCH A POOR PHYSIQUE, AT THAT!
ER-- THINK SO?
HE'S GOT SOME GOOD BASIC MATERIAL THERE, BUT IT'S GOT TO BE WHIPPED INTO SHAPE. PUT ON THESE GLOVES!

OUCH! THAT HURT!!

BUT CLARK SKILLFULLY DODGES MIKE'S POWER-HOUSE PUNCHES, AND THE INFURIATED PHYSICAL INSTRUCTOR CONTINUALLY FLAILS EMPTY SPACE...!
FIGHT LIKE A MAN, YA CRAZY JACK-IN-TH'-BOX!!
DISCRETION IS THE BETTER PART OF VALOR!
9

YOW-W!
TCH! TCH!
I'VE SEEN ENOUGH OF THIS FARCE! WHILE YOU TWO PLAY HIDE-AND-GO SEEK, I'VE IMPORTANT WORK TO DO!

I'M CLARK KENT. CAN YOU TELL ME WHO THAT FELLOW IS?
HE'S NAT FOLSOM, A BANKER. BUT THEY SAY HE MADE HIS FORTUNE OUT OF PROHIBITION. ME, I'M JAKE MASSEY, JUST AN ORDINARY GUY.

DOES ANYTHING--ER--UNUSUAL--THAT IS, OTHER THAN GYM INSTRUCTION, GO ON AROUND HERE? ("-SO FOLSOM MAY HAVE BEEN A RACKETEER!-")
THE ONLY THING I'VE NOTICED IS THAT THEY EXERCISE YOU TO TH' POINT OF EXHAUSTION. IT'S TOO MUCH FOR ME. I'M THINKING OF QUITTING!

MEANWHILE--AS MIKE BANDAGES HIS BRUISED FIST IN HIS PRIVATE OFFICE....
BLAST THAT KENT! I'LL MAKE HIM PAY FOR MAKING ME LOOK LIKE A SAP BEFORE HIS GIRL!
YOU'LL DO NOTHING OF THE KIND, MIKE!

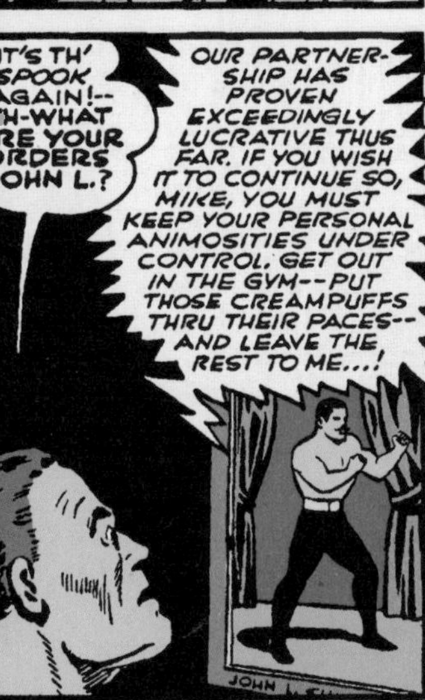

IT'S TH' SPOOK AGAIN!--TH-WHAT ARE YOUR ORDERS JOHN L.?
OUR PARTNERSHIP HAS PROVEN EXCEEDINGLY LUCRATIVE THUS FAR. IF YOU WISH IT TO CONTINUE SO, MIKE, YOU MUST KEEP YOUR PERSONAL ANIMOSITIES UNDER CONTROL. GET OUT IN THE GYM--PUT THOSE CREAMPUFFS THRU THEIR PACES--AND LEAVE THE REST TO ME...!

MIKE PUTS HIS CLIENTS THRU A GRUELING SET OF EXERCISES.
PUSH-UPS...!
FASTER YOU DECREPIT DODOS!
MEDICINE-BALL BARRAGE!
HARDER! THIS AIN'T BEAN BAG!
WRESTLING...!
HELP! I'M STUCK!

SO THAT HALF AN HOUR LATER, MIKE'S CUSTOMERS LAY WINDED AND PANTING ON THE MATS... AND AS THEY RECLINE THERE, HALF CONSCIOUS, COMPLETELY EXHAUSTED, A COMMANDING VOICE BOOMS FORTH....
STRONG! STRONG! ALL OF YOU ARE DARING, SUPERB ATHLETES--AND COMPLETELY SUBJECT TO MY WILL!
SUPERB ATHLETES--SUBJECT TO YOUR WILL...
("-MASS HYPNOTISM! I'LL PRETEND TO BE HYPNOTIZED WITH THE OTHERS!-")

YOU WHO CALL YOURSELF CLARK KENT--YOU ARE NOW SUPERMAN! YOU POSSESS ALL HIS MIGHTY POWERS!
HERE. PUT ON THIS SPECIALLY MADE SUPERMAN UNIFORM.
("-WHAT A LAUGH! THEY'RE TRYING TO HYPNOTIZE ME INTO THINKING I'M SUPERMAN AND THE JOKE OF IT IS--I AM!-")

AFTER CLARK DONS THE UNIFORM....
UNDERSTAND? YOU ARE NOW ALL-POWERFUL! YOUR STRENGTH IS TERRIFIC!
LIKE THIS?
HOLY COW! HE SOCKED CLEAR THRU TH' WALL!

AN' TH' MIRACLE OF IT IS, HE DIDN'T BREAK A BONE, OR GET A SCRATCH!
WHAT ELSE DO YOU EXPECT OF SUPERMAN?
ATTENTION! YOUR INSTRUCTIONS ARE TO LOOT A BAZAAR BEING HELD AT THE HOTEL HANSOM'S PENTHOUSE BALLROOM THIS AFTERNOON. BRING THE LOOT HERE--THEN--FORGET EVERYTHING!!!

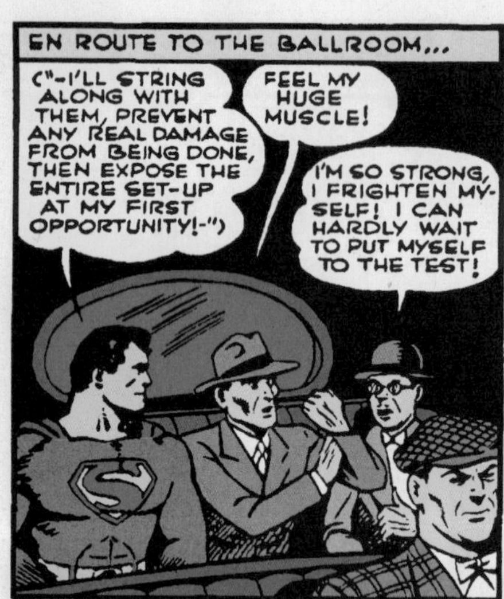

EN ROUTE TO THE BALLROOM...
("-I'LL STRING ALONG WITH THEM, PREVENT ANY REAL DAMAGE FROM BEING DONE, THEN EXPOSE THE ENTIRE SET-UP AT MY FIRST OPPORTUNITY!-")
FEEL MY HUGE MUSCLE!
I'M SO STRONG, I FRIGHTEN MY-SELF! I CAN HARDLY WAIT TO PUT MYSELF TO THE TEST!

MEANWHILE--LOIS IS COVERING THE BAZAAR FOR THE SOCIETY PAGE...
HERE'S WHERE THINGS PICK UP! SUPERMAN!

BUT IN THE ENSUING MOMENTS IT IS CLEAR THAT THE NEW ARRIVALS HAVE COME FOR BUT ONE PURPOSE--ROBBERY!
BUT SURELY YOU WON'T STAND IDLY BY AND PERMIT THIS!
SHE SQUAWKS TOO MUCH! I GOTTA GOOD MIND TO SHOOT HER DOWN!
NO. LET'S TAKE HER BACK TO THE GYM AND DECIDE THERE WHAT HER FATE IS TO BE!
("-I'VE HAD PLENTY OF SCOOPS LATELY. IT'S ABOUT TIME I GAVE LOIS A BREAK!-")
BUT AS THE MESMERIZED BANDITS DEPART, SUPERMAN RACES BACK WITH THE LOOT-BURDENED SACK AT TOP SPEED....
NOW FOR A REFUND!
RACING SO SWIFTLY THE CANNOT FOLLOW HIS MOV MENTS, HE REPLACES THE LOOT IN THE POCKETS O THE ROBBERY-VICTIMS..
CRIME TAKES A HOLIDAY!

AND A FRACTION OF A MOMENT LATER HE IS BACK WITH THE ESCAPING BANDITS....
("-WOULD MY PARTNERS IN CRIME BE ASTONISHED TO LEARN THAT THE SACK IS FILLED WITH CHEAP DECORATIONS!-")
11

BACK IN THE PENTHOUSE BALL-ROOM....
WHA--? BUT I DISTINCTLY REMEMBER MY WATCH HAVING BEEN STOLEN!
MY BRACELET!
AND TO THINK I SWORE OFF DRINKING THIS MORNING!

LATER--AT THE MUSCLE ORIUM....
COUNT THE LOOT!
HUH? NOTHIN' HERE BUT CHEAP BAZAAR DECORATION MATERIALS!

WHAT SORT
F A DOUBLE-
ROSSER'S
RICK IS THIS?
CUT IT OUT, MASSEY, OR THE SPOOK OF JOHN L. SULLIVAN WILL TAKE CARE OF YOU!
("-HERE'S WHERE THINGS START POPPING!-")

YOU FOOL--THERE NEVER WAS A GHOST! AN ACCOMPLISHED HYPNOTIST, I PLACED MINIATURE RADIO-EQUIPMENT BEHIND EACH OF THE PICTURES, AND BROADCAST MY MESSAGES THRU THIS SMALL MICROPHONE. I KNEW THAT YOUR CLIENTS ALL DESIRED TO BE STRONG MEN AND THAT THEY WOULD BE EASY SUBJECTS FOR HYPNOTISM--MY IDEA TO HAVE THESE FRUSTRATED PHYSICAL WRECKS PULL DARING ROBBERIES WHILE UNDER THE INFLUENCE OF HYPNOTISM WAS SUCCESSFUL, BUT I NEVER COUNTED ON YOU DOUBLE-CROSSING ME!

BUT I DIDN'T DOUBLE-CROSS YA, CHIEF!
YOU'RE LYING!
ON THE CONTRARY, THE CREDIT IS ENTIRELY MINE!

RUSH HIM! CRUSH HIM! I COMMAND YOU!
HOW TO OVERCOME THEM--WITHOUT HARMING THEM--??
THEY SHOULD KNOW THEY HAVEN'T A CHANCE AGAINST SUPERMAN!
BUT THAT'S NOT SUPERMAN--THAT'S YOUR REPORTER FRIEND, CLARK KENT, MADE UP TO LOOK LIKE HIM!

AN INSPIRATION STRIKES THE MAN OF STEEL. SNATCHING UP SEVERAL EXERCISE-CABLES, HE LINKS THEM TOGETHER ABOUT THE CHARGING MEN, EFFECTIVELY IMPRISONING THEM....
THERE! THAT OUGHT TO HOLD YOU!
TAKE HIM, MIKE!
WITH PLEASURE!

THE PLEASURE IS ALL MINE!
OOOO-OOF!
NICE GOING!
AWK!

SCRAMBLING ERECT, MASSEY DRAWS A BEAD ON LOIS....
AT LEAST I'LL GET YOUR GIRL FRIEND!
NO YOU WON'T!

ABRUPTLY, MASSEY DUCKS--OUT THE WINDOW TOPPLES SUPERMAN!
LOOK OUT!
THE END OF THAT FOOL!

AND NOW TO FINISH YOU!
NO— DON'T--!
HA! HA! TOO BAD YOUR BOY FRIEND CAN'T HELP YOU NOW!
ROUND TRIP!
LAST STOP --SWITCH TO EXPRESS, PLEASE!
BACK AGAIN! BUT HOW--??!
IS IT POSSIBLE THAT MY HYPNOTIC SUGGESTION REALLY GAVE YOU SUPERMAN'S MIGHTY POWERS?
COME, COME, BOYS! DON'T TELL ME YOU HAVEN'T YET REALIZED THAT I FREED CLARK KENT FROM THE HYPNOTIC SPELL AND TOOK HIS PLACE LONG AGO!
NO WONDER I THOUGHT YOU WERE SUPERMAN ALL ALONG!
AND IF YOU'RE STILL DOUBTFUL-- HERE'S PROOF!
FREEING THE GYM CLIENTS FROM THEIR BONDS AND THE HYPNOTIC TRANCE, SUPERMAN SPRINGS AWAY....
I WANT ALL OF YOU MEN TO MEET ME AT PELHAM'S PLATEAU ONE WEEK FROM TODAY!
WE'LL BE THERE!
13
NEXT DAY--
YOU'RE SCOOPED— MR. BRANT HAS BEEN RESTORED TO HIS SENSES AND FREED—ALL THE LOOT STOLEN IN THE ROBBERIES HAS BEEN RETURNED—MIKE MOSBY AND JAKE MASSEY HAVE RECEIVED LONG JAIL TERMS! I FEEL SWELL!
WHAT CHANCE HAS AN ORDINARY GUY LIKE ME AGAINST A SUPERMAN?
SIX DAYS LATER-- PELHAM'S PLATEAU....
THERE YOU ARE, GENTLEMEN! JUST FOLLOW THE FEW SIMPLE RULES I'VE MENTIONED AND YOU'LL SOON BE IN TIP-TOP SHAPE!
I FEEL BETTER ALREADY
IT ISN'T EVERYON WHO CAN HA SUPERMA GIVE HIM PERSONA LESSONS I BODY-BUILDING
THE EN

10¢
SUPERMAN
DC
NATIONAL COMICS
JUNE
NO. 241
APPROVED BY THE COMICS CODE AUTHORITY
ACTION COMICS
Featuring
"The SUPER-KEY to FORT SUPERMAN!"
IT WOULD TAKE ONE HUNDRED MEN TO LIFT THIS SUPER-KEY--YET SOMEONE HAS MANAGED TO USE IT! WHO COULD IT BE?
FORT SUPERMA

SUPERMAN
REG U S PAT OFF
JUNE 10
TODAY I WILL BEGIN THE MOST DARING EXPERIMENT OF MY LIFE! IT IS SO DANGEROUS THAT I WILL USE A LANGUAGE NO ONE ELSE IN THE UNIVERSE KNOWS ..THE LANGUAGE OF MY DESTROYED NATIVE PLANET, KRYPTON!
MY DIARY
DEEP IN THE CORE OF A MOUNTAINSIDE IN THE DESOLATE ARCTIC WASTES LIES SUPERMAN'S FORTRESS OF SOLITUDE, WHERE THE MAN OF STEEL CONDUCTS INCREDIBLE EXPERIMENTS, KEEPS STRANGE TROPHIES, AND PURSUES ASTOUNDING HOBBIES! ITS CONTENTS WILL AMAZE YOU... BUT EVEN MORE AMAZING IS THE IMPOSSIBLE ENIGMA BEHIND THE INTRUDER WHO FOUND A WAY TO USE—
The SUPER-KEY TO FORT SUPERMAN

ONE DAY AS CLARK KENT, SECRETLY SUPERMAN, GOES OUT FOR LUNCH WITH HIS REPORTER FRIENDS, LOIS LANE ND JIMMY OLSEN...
I'VE BEEN WANTING A ECKLACE LIKE THAT ALL MY LIFE, BUT (SIGH) I KNOW 'LL NEVER GET IT.
OH, DON'T BE SO SURE. YOU MAY, ONE DAY.

YEAH--SHE'LL GET IT-- THE SAME DAY I GET THAT SPORTS CAR I'VE BEEN DREAMING ABOUT!
EXACTLY, JIMMY... BUT I CAN'T TELL YOU WHEN...OR HOW!
Imported Custom SPORT CARS


ATER THAT DAY, WHEN HIS EPORTER'S WORK IS DONE, MILD-MANNERED CLARK DOFFS HIS UTER CLOTHING AND IS TRANSFORMED TO SUPERMAN!

I HAVE THE REST OF THE DAY FREE, SO I MAY AS WELL WORK ON THOSE GIFTS NOW... AND PAY A LITTLE VISIT I'VE BEEN LOOKING FORWARD TO!

SOON AFTERWARD, THE MAN OF STEEL PROBES A SEA-BED OF OYSTERS WITH HIS X-RAY VISION...

AAAH... ANOTHER PEARL FOR LOIS' NECKLACE! I'VE SALVAGED ENOUGH TO WORK WITH! NOW TO GET TO MY DESTINATION!

STREAKING NORTHWARD AT METEOR-SPEED, SUPERMAN SOON STANDS ON A ESOLATE MOUNTAIN TOP IN THE ARCTIC...

FROM ABOVE, THIS LOOKS LIKE A LUMINOUS ARROW MARKER TO GUIDE PLANES OVER THIS LONELY REGION! NO ONE WOULD SUSPECT IT'S REALLY A KEY-- A SUPER-KEY THAT EIGHS TONS--AND THAT O ONE ELSE CAN LIFT!

SOON, THE MAN OF STEEL FITS THE PONDEROUS KEY INTO A MASSIVE DOOR SHELTERED FROM VIEW BY JUTTING ROCKS...

AND THE GIANT KEY FITS INTO A GIGANTIC DOOR SO HEAVY THAT NO HUMAN ON EARTH COULD MOVE IT AN INCH!

2

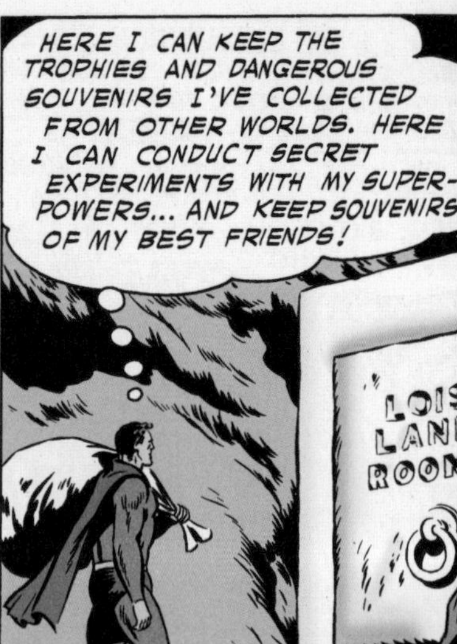

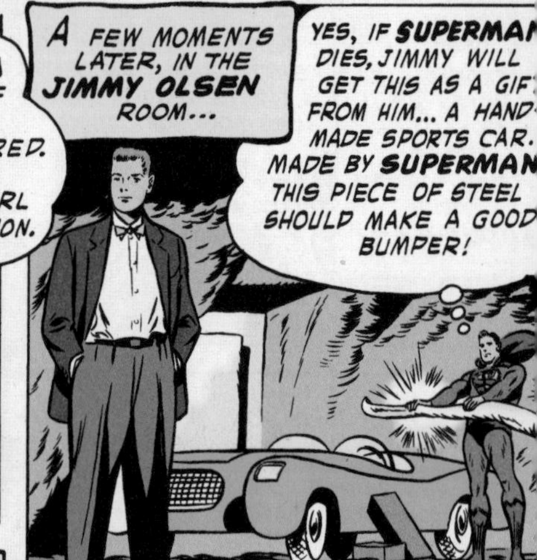


LATER, IN THE ROOM SUPERMAN HAS BUILT IN HONOR OF HIS CRIME-FIGHTING FRIEND, THE BATMAN...

THIS "ROBOT DETECTIVE" SHOULD HELP BATMAN... IF EVER I CAN'T HELP HIM ANY MORE! WE'VE WORKED TOGETHER ON MANY CASE IN THE PAST... LIKE THE "BAD PENNY CRIMES" OF THE JOKER, AND BATMAN'S THE ONE PERSON I CA TRUST WITH ALL MY SECRETS!

LIGHTNING FINGERPRINT CLASSIFIER

ELECTRONIC CLUE ANALYSIS

CRIME PROBABILITY PREDICTER

THE BAD PENNY
GOOD FOR ONE CRIME JOKER

PRESENTLY, IN STILL ANOTHER CHAMBER OF THIS UNDERGROUND LABYRINTH OF WONDERS...
I'VE EVEN MADE A CLARK KENT ROOM! CLARK IS KNOWN TO BE A FRIEND OF SUPERMAN, AND IF SOME UNEXPECTED EARTHQUAKE EVER OPENED MY SECRET CAVE TO A STRANGER THAT WAX CLARK WOULD HELP PRESERVE THE SECRET OF MY IDENTITY!

AND, EVEN A SUPERMAN MUST HAVE HOBBIES... OR SUPER-HOBBIES!
NOW TO ENJOY SOME PAINTING! THIS ISN'T THE RESULT OF MY IMAGINATION -- IT'S A REALISTIC PICTURE OF A MARTIAN LANDSCAPE, AS OBSERVED BY MY TELESCOPIC VISION!

YES, IT'S A BUSY, PLEASANT VISIT FOR SUPERMAN AS HE WINDS UP THE DAY WITH AN IMPORTANT EXPERIMENT!
IN THIS LEAD ARMOR, I'M IMMUNE TO KRYPTONITE RAYS... AND CAN STUDY IT TO SEE IF I CAN OVERCOME ITS DANGEROUS EFFECT ON ME. WHEN I'VE FINISHED EXPERIMENTING, I'LL PUT IT BACK IN A LEAD CONTAINER.

FINALLY, THE MAN OF STEEL PAYS A RELUCTANT FAREWELL TO HIS MOUNTAIN FORTRESS OF SILENCE AND SOLITUDE...

WHAT A WONDERFUL NIGHT! IT'S NOT OFTEN I GET TIME TO MYSELF...TIME WHICH I CAN USE FOR MY HOBBIES AND SELF-IMPROVEMENT!

NEXT DAY, AS SUPERMAN RESPONDS TO AN URGENT CALL FROM A FAMOUS SCIENTIST...
I'VE CREATED A METAL WHICH I THINK EVEN YOU CAN'T BREAK! PLEASE TRY IT OUT IN SOME ISOLATED PLACE. I'M AFRAID REVERBERATIONS MAY SHATTER BUILDINGS IF YOU HIT IT WITH ALL YOUR STRENGTH!
GOOD! IT GIVES ME AN EXCUSE TO PAY ANOTHER VISIT TO MY HIDEOUT!

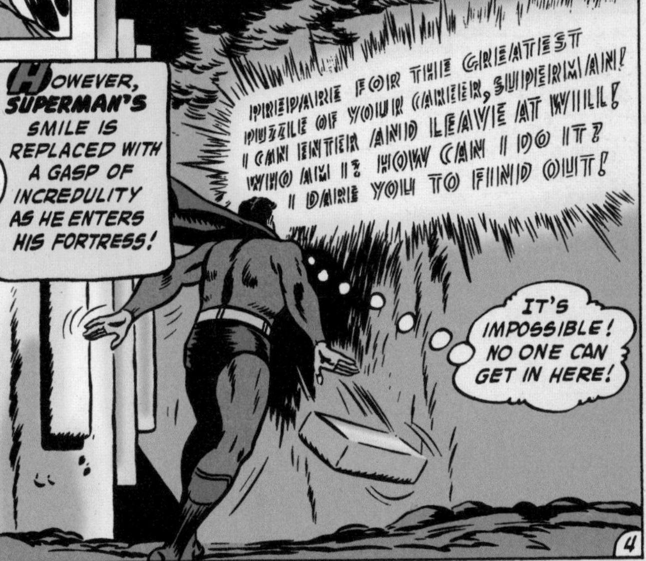
HOWEVER, SUPERMAN'S SMILE IS REPLACED WITH A GASP OF INCREDULITY AS HE ENTERS HIS FORTRESS!
PREPARE FOR THE GREATEST PUZZLE OF YOUR CAREER, SUPERMAN! I CAN ENTER AND LEAVE AT WILL! WHO AM I? HOW CAN I DO IT? I DARE YOU TO FIND OUT!
IT'S IMPOSSIBLE! NO ONE CAN GET IN HERE!
4

NO OTHER PERSON COULD HAVE LIFTED THAT KEY OR MOVED THE DOOR! AND WHO COULD PLUNGE THROUGH FIFTY FEET OF SOLID ROCK... THE ONLY OTHER WAY IN? I'LL CHECK MY TROPHIES! SOME OF THEM MIGHT PROVIDE A CLUE!
TROPHY TAKEN WHILE SOLVING LUTHOR'S "JACK-IN-THE-BOX" CRIMES

SOON, IN A HEAVILY BARRED ROOM...
THOSE BUBBLING COLORED CRYSTALS FROM PLANET X... IS IT POSSIBLE THEY RELEASED SOME ALIEN, POWERFUL FORM OF LIFE THAT'S MOCKING ME? HMM... I WONDER!

MOMENTS LATER, THE MAN OF STEEL ENTERS ANOTHER LOCKED CHAMBER...
THESE "PETS" FROM OTHER WORLDS... PART OF MY INTERPLANETARY ZOO. HAS ONE OF THEM BEEN CONCEALING SUPERHUMAN POWERS AND INTELLIGENCE? I MUST BE CAREFUL... THE VERY SAFETY OF EARTH ITSELF MAY BE AT STAKE!

SO, SUPERMAN WALKS THROUGH HIS STRANGE FORTRESS, EXAMINING EVERY NOOK AND CRANNY!
THAT STRANGE APPARATUS MADE BY LUTHOR, THE CUNNING SCIENTIFIC GENIUS! IT WAS SUPPOSED TO SUMMON BEINGS FROM THE FOURTH DIMENSION! HAS SOME UNDERGROUND VIBRATION STARTED IT, AND MADE IT WORK?
FORBIDDEN WEAPONS OF CRIMEDOM

I HAVE LOTS OF THEORIES... BUT NO EVIDENCE! WELL, I'LL GIVE "MR. X" ENOUGH ROPE SO THAT HE MAY BETRAY HIMSELF. IN THE MEANWHILE, I'LL GO AHEAD WITH MY PLANS FOR TONIGHT AND TEST THAT SHATTERPROOF METAL!
THE BAD PENNY
GOOD FOR ONE CRIME
JOKER
TROPHY OF JOINT SUPERMAN-BATMAN ATTACK ON CRIME

PRESENTLY, SUPERMAN DRIVES HIS IGHTY FIST AT THE METAL, AND...
I'M AFRAID THE PROFESSOR'S METAL IS NOT SO SHATTERPROOF AS HE THINKS! I'LL HAVE TO PATCH THAT WALL, AND THEN MAKE A FEW ENTRIES IN MY DIARY!
WHAMMMP!

THERE'S NO CHANCE MY DIARY WILL EVER BE DESTROYED! THE PAGES ARE MADE OF METAL AND I ENGRAVE ALL MY ENTRIES WITH MY FINGERNAILS!
AND THERE'S NO DANGER THAT ANYONE WILL EVER READ THESE PAGES. I WRITE EVERYTHING IN KRYPTONESE, THE LANGUAGE OF THE PLANET ON WHICH I WAS BORN!
LATER, AFTER SUPERMAN LEAVES, AND LOCKS THE PONDEROUS DOOR THAT LEADS TO HIS FORTRESS...
IT'S JUST POSSIBLE SOMEONE FOUND MY KEY AND WAS ABLE TO LIFT IT SOMEHOW! I'LL USE THE HEAT OF MY X-RAY VISION TO MELT THE DOOR AND FUSE IT INTO THE ROCK OF THE MOUNTAIN! THEN THERE WILL BE NO ENTRANCE!

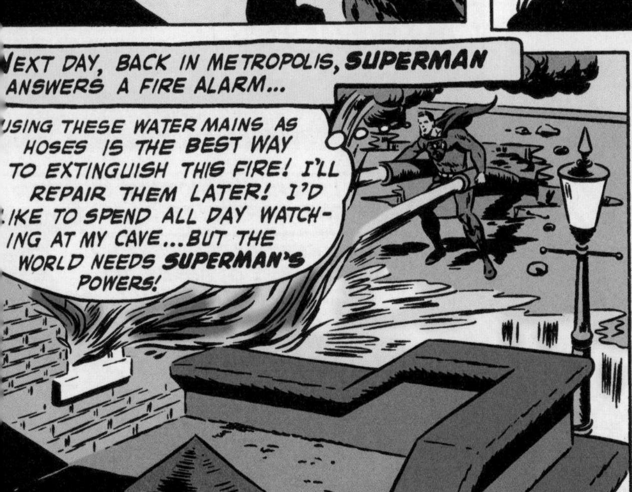
NEXT DAY, BACK IN METROPOLIS, SUPERMAN ANSWERS A FIRE ALARM...
USING THESE WATER MAINS AS HOSES IS THE BEST WAY TO EXTINGUISH THIS FIRE! I'LL REPAIR THEM LATER! I'D LIKE TO SPEND ALL DAY WATCHING AT MY CAVE...BUT THE WORLD NEEDS SUPERMAN'S POWERS!

AND, THAT EVENING, WHEN HIS SUPER-WORK IS DONE, SUPERMAN SPEEDS TO HIS ARCTIC RETREAT, WHERE...
THERE'S ONLY ONE WAY TO GET IN NOW... AND I CAN'T WAIT TILL I DO!
6

SOMEONE COMPLETED THAT PAINTING I'D STARTED! BUT IT'S **NOT** A MARTIAN LANDSCAPE! I'VE NEVER SEEN ANYTHING LIKE THAT... IN ALL MY TRAVELS THROUGH THE SOLAR SYSTEM! IT'S WEIRD-- UTTERLY WEIRD!

LATER, AS A BEWILDERED **SUPERMAN** RELAXES BY PLAYING SUPER-CHESS WITH A GREAT ROBOT HE HAS BUILT AS A PLAYMATE FOR HIMSELF...

THIS ROBOT POSSESSES A SUPER-ELECTRONIC BRAIN! HE CAN THINK AND PLAY WITH THE SPEED OF LIGHTNING, AND PLANS A MILLION MOVES AT ONCE! IT'S TOUGH BEATING HIM!

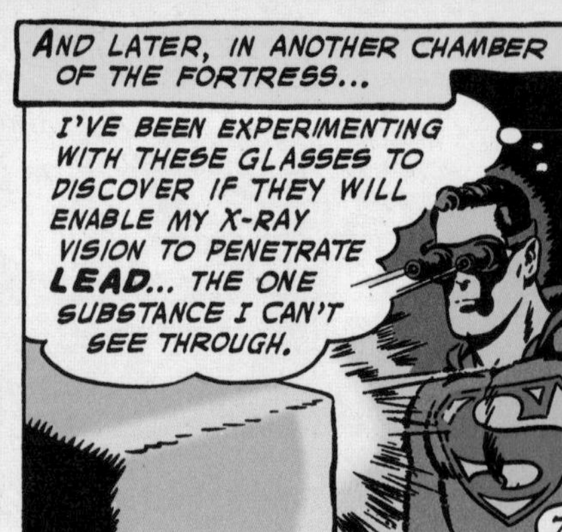

MOMENTS LATER, AS SUPERMAN TURNS ON THE FULL FORCE OF HIS X-RAY VISION...
WRITING IS APPEARING ON THAT LEAD SHEET! IT...IT MUST HAVE BEEN DONE IN INVISIBLE INK WHICH THE HEAT BROUGHT OUT! I'D WRITTEN IN MY DIARY THAT I PLANNED THIS EXPERIMENT TODAY! "MR. X" MUST HAVE READ IT! BUT HOW COULD HE UNDERSTAND KRYPTONESE?
I TOLD YOU I COULDN OUT! YOU LIKE PUZZLE GUESS WHO I AM?
THIS IS THE CLEVEREST, MOST CUNNING OPPONENT I'VE EVER FACED! WHO AND WHAT CAN HE BE? IF HE KNOWS MY IDENTITY, I'LL BE COMPLETELY AT HIS MERCY!
I TOLD YOU I COULDN'T BE KEPT OUT! YOU LIKE PUZZLES! CAN YOU GUESS WHO I AM? I KNOW WHO YOU ARE...AND I'LL REVEAL MY KNOWLEDGE IN 24 HOURS!
SOMEWHAT LATER...
I COULD RETURN THESE CREATURES TO THEIR NATIVE WORLDS... BUT IF ONE OF THEM POSSESSES SUPER-INTELLIGENCE, IT COULD RETURN! I...I'LL JUST HAVE TO WAIT... WAIT UNTIL MY UNKNOWN FOE SHOWS HIS HAND!
THAT NIGHT, AS CLARK SLEEPS IN HIS APARTMENT, WEIRD NIGHTMARES TROUBLE HIS SLUMBER...
YOUR DAYS ARE NUMBERED, SUPERMAN! I KNOW YOUR IDENTITY, AND I WILL CHASE YOU FROM EARTH FOREVER!
NO! NO!
AND, NEXT DAY, AS SUPERMAN RESUMES HIS SUPER-CHORES AND FLIES A DISABLED SHIP HOME TO PORT...
SUPERMAN! WATCH OUT!
WH-WHAT?
Y-YOU'RE ROCKING THE BOAT! THIS VOYAGE IS MORE DANGEROUS THAN THE ONE YOU RESCUED US FROM!
I'M (GULP) SORRY!
I CAN'T CONCENTRATE ON ANYTHING ELSE... EXCEPT THE INTRUDER! I WISH IT WERE NIGHT...SO I COULD GO BACK TO MY FORTRESS!
8

THAT EVENING, SUPERMAN SPEEDS NORTHWARD AND PLUNGES INTO THE ROCK ROOF OF HIS FORTRESS...
IF THE INTRUDER KNOWS THE SECRET OF MY IDENTITY, IT MAY MEAN THE END OF MY CAREER! I HAVE A FEELING THAT TONIGHT WE WILL COME FACE TO FACE!
WHAMMP!
ONCE INSIDE, SUPERMAN GRIMLY STALKS FROM ONE CHAMBER TO THE NEXT, UNTIL...
INCREDIBLE! WHO-- OR WHAT IS HE? I... I MUST THINK... MUST SEARCH FOR AT LEAST ONE CLUE!
KENT IS SUPERMA I TOLD YOU I KNE NOW I HAVE PROVED IT! TONIGHT IS YOU LAST CHANCE TO ACT
AS THE MAN OF STEEL COMBS EVERY INCH OF HIS VAST CAVERN FOR A LEAD...
GOOD FOR ONE CRIME THE JOKER
A BLOB OF MELTED WAX ON THE FLOOR... GREY AND BLUE! I... I CAN'T BELIEVE IT... BUT THAT MUST BE THE EXPLANATION! NOW, IT'S MY TURN TO ACT! BUT FIRST, I MUST CHECK MY THEORY AND EXAMINE THE GIANT KEY I USED TO GET IN!
MEANWHILE...
HA, HA! SUPERMAN HAS NOT GUESSED WHO I AM... OR HOW I GOT IN! WHEN RETURNS, I WILL REVEA MYSELF, AND HE'LL GET T SHOCK OF HIS LIFE!
HOWEVER, A MOMENT LATER...
THE WALLS OF THIS FORTRESS ARE SHAKING! IT'S AN EARTHQUAKE!
AND, WHEN SUPERMAN RETURNS...
GREAT SCOTT! I'LL NEVER BE ABLE TO GET OUT OF HERE ALIVE! I'M SEALED IN BY TONS OF ROCKS! AND SUPERMAN CAN'T HELP ME, EITHER-- THE QUAKE DISLODGED THAT CHUNK OF KRYPTONITE HE WAS WORKING ON!

FOR LONG MOMENTS, SUPERMAN LIES SILENT, AND THEN...
DON'T WORRY, SUPERMAN! I'LL SAVE YOU!
BATMAN! Y-YOU... ARE THE... INTRUDER!
YES! IT WAS ALL A JEST TO AMUSE YOU. I'LL EXPLAIN EVERYTHING AS SOON AS I TAKE THIS KRYPTONITE AWAY!
IT'S NO USE, OLD FRIEND. YOU CAN'T-- TAKE IT OUT OF THIS ROOM-- AND NO MATTER WHERE YOU TAKE IT IN THE ROOM-- IT STILL WEAKENS ME!
A MOMENT LATER, THE GRIM TRUTH DAWNS ON BATMAN AS...
WE'RE SEALED IN BY TONS OF ROCK! THE ONLY WAY OUT OF THIS CAVE IS WITH YOUR SUPER-STRENGTH, AND YOU'LL NEVER BE ABLE TO USE IT BECAUSE OF THE KRYPTONITE LOCKED IN HERE WITH US!
YES, BATMAN. IT'S THE END... FOR BOTH OF US! I'M WEAKENING RAPIDLY...
I'M SORRY YOU ARE THE INTRUDER, BECAUSE IT MEANS YOU MUST SHARE MY DOOM. HOWEVER, LET US FACE OUR FATE BRAVELY. AS OUR LAST MINUTES DRAW TO AN END, TELL ME... HOW DID YOU GET IN... AND WHY?
VERY WELL, SUPERMAN!
REMEMBER THE DAY, YEARS AGO, WHEN I TOLD YOU THAT MY SECRET IDENTITY WAS BRUCE WAYNE, AND ADMITTED YOU TO THE BAT-CAVE? YOU TOLD ME THEN THAT YOU WERE CLARK KENT...
OF COURSE! AND I TOLD YOU ABOUT MY FORTRESS! I... I NEVER SUSPECTED YOU BECAUSE I TRUSTED YOU SO COMPLETELY.
10

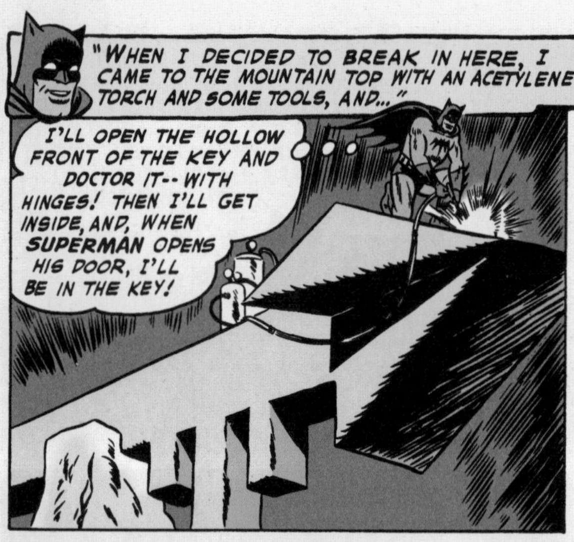
"WHEN I DECIDED TO BREAK IN HERE, I CAME TO THE MOUNTAIN TOP WITH AN ACETYLENE TORCH AND SOME TOOLS, AND..."
I'LL OPEN THE HOLLOW FRONT OF THE KEY AND DOCTOR IT-- WITH HINGES! THEN I'LL GET INSIDE, AND, WHEN SUPERMAN OPENS HIS DOOR, I'LL BE IN THE KEY!

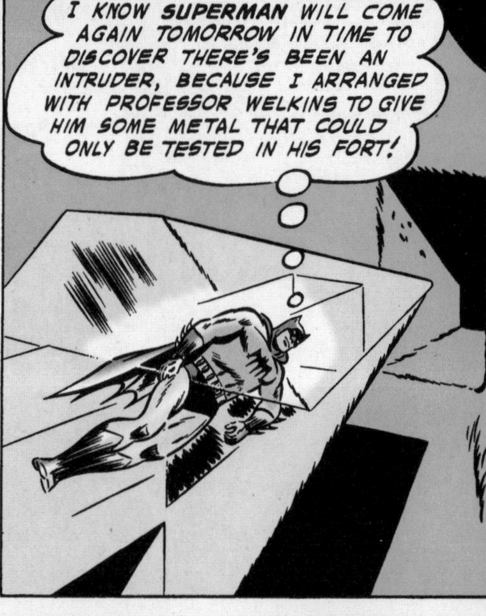
"MY PLAN WORKED PERFECTLY!"
I KNOW SUPERMAN WILL COME AGAIN TOMORROW IN TIME TO DISCOVER THERE'S BEEN AN INTRUDER, BECAUSE I ARRANGED WITH PROFESSOR WELKINS TO GIVE HIM SOME METAL THAT COULD ONLY BE TESTED IN HIS FORT!

"WHILE YOU WERE BUSY, I SLIPPED OUT OF THE KEY AND HID. THEN, WHEN YOU LEFT..."
I KNEW THIS "BAD PENNY" WAS ONE OF SUPERMAN'S TROPHIES... SINCE WE WORKED ON THE CASE TOGETHER! AND, AS IT'S MADE OF LEAD WHICH HIS X-RAY VISION CAN'T PIERCE, ITS INTERIOR WILL BE A PERFECT HIDING PLACE! WHAT A PUZZLE I'LL GIVE HIM!
THE BAD PENNY

"EARLIER TONIGHT I MELTED DOWN THE WAX FIGURE OF YOU IN THE "BATMAN ROOM" WITH A FLARE FROM MY UTILITY BELT..."

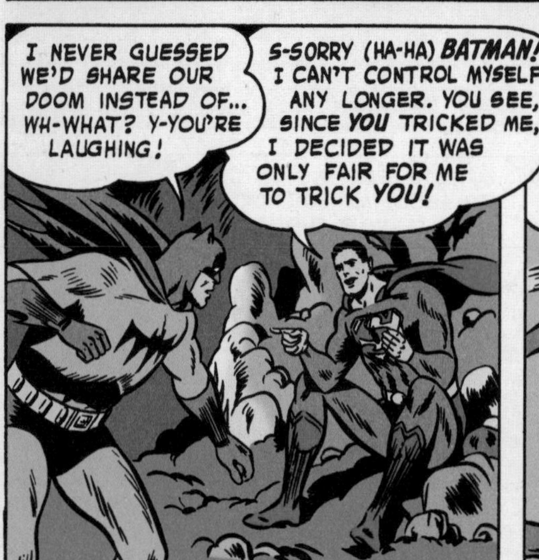
I NEVER GUESSED WE'D SHARE OUR DOOM INSTEAD OF... WH-WHAT? Y-YOU'RE LAUGHING!
S-SORRY (HA-HA) BATMAN! I CAN'T CONTROL MYSELF ANY LONGER. YOU SEE, SINCE YOU TRICKED ME, I DECIDED IT WAS ONLY FAIR FOR ME TO TRICK YOU!

SUDDENLY, THE MAN OF STEEL LEAPS UP, AND...
THAT KRYPTONITE IS PHONY AND THE 'QUAKE WAS CAUSED BY VIBRATIONS FROM A SUPER-CLAP OF MY HANDS. THE REST OF THE FORT IS STILL UNHARMED!

WHEN I SAW THAT BLOB OF WAX, I REALIZED THAT SOMEONE HAD MELTED DOWN THE GREY AND BLUE WAX FIGURE OF BATMAN! YET, THE "STATUE" WAS STILL THERE! I REALIZED THEN THAT BATMAN WAS HERE IN THE FLESH AND HAD REPLACED THE WAX FIGURE OF HIMSELF!
THE JOKER
HMM... I LEFT MY HIDING PLACE IN THE COIN, BECAUSE I WAS READY TO SURPRISE YOU WITH THE SOLUTION IF YOU DIDN'T GET IT YOURSELF TONIGHT!
AS SOON AS I REALIZED IT WAS YOU, I CHECKED THE KEY AND SAW HOW YOU GOT IN. THEN I PLANNED A LITTLE SURPRISE FOR YOU!
ONLY ONE THING STILL PUZZLES ME, OLD FRIEND. WHY DID YOU PLAY THIS TRICK ON ME?
YOU MAY NOT RECALL IT, BUT TODAY IS THE ANNIVERSARY OF YOUR ARRIVAL ON EARTH FROM THE PLANET KRYPTON! I WONDERED FOR A LONG TIME WHAT TO GET YOU AS A GIFT! WHAT CAN ONE GET FOR A SUPERMAN?
"I LOOKED AT ALL THE STORES FOR IDEAS, AND THEN..."
THAT'S IT! A PUZZLE! ONE THAT EVEN SUPERMAN WILL FIND IT HARD TO SOLVE!
A good puzzle makes a GOOD GIFT
PUZZLE
THANKS, PAL! YOU GAVE ME A GIFT THAT I'LL REMEMBER FOR THE REST OF MY LIFE!
AND YOU GAVE ME A SCARE I'LL REMEMBER FOREVER! NOW, I WANT YOU TO JOIN ME IN THE BAT-CAVE!
LATER, THAT EVENING...
I BAKED IT MYSELF. I HOPE YOU DON'T NEED SUPER-STRENGTH TO CUT IT!
DON'T WORRY. I CAN EAT SOLID STEEL!
SUPERMA
Happy Anniversary
The End

SUPERMAN
DC
NATIONAL COMICS
10¢
FEB.
NO. 261
APPROVED
BY THE
COMICS
CODE
AUTHORITY
ACTION
REG. U.S. PAT. OFF.
COMICS
Featuring
"SECRETS OF THE FORTRESS OF SOLITUDE!"
DEATH TO SUPERMAN!
WIPE HIM OUT!
DESTROY HIM!
GREAT SCOTT! AN EVIL FORCE HAS CAUSED THE WAX DUMMIES OF LOIS, JIMMY, JOR-EL AND PERRY IN MY FORTRESS TO COME TO LIFE! NOW THEY, TOO, HAVE SUPER-POWERS!
LOIS LANE
JOR
RY WHITE
Extra! MEET SUPERGIRL'S SUPER-CAT!

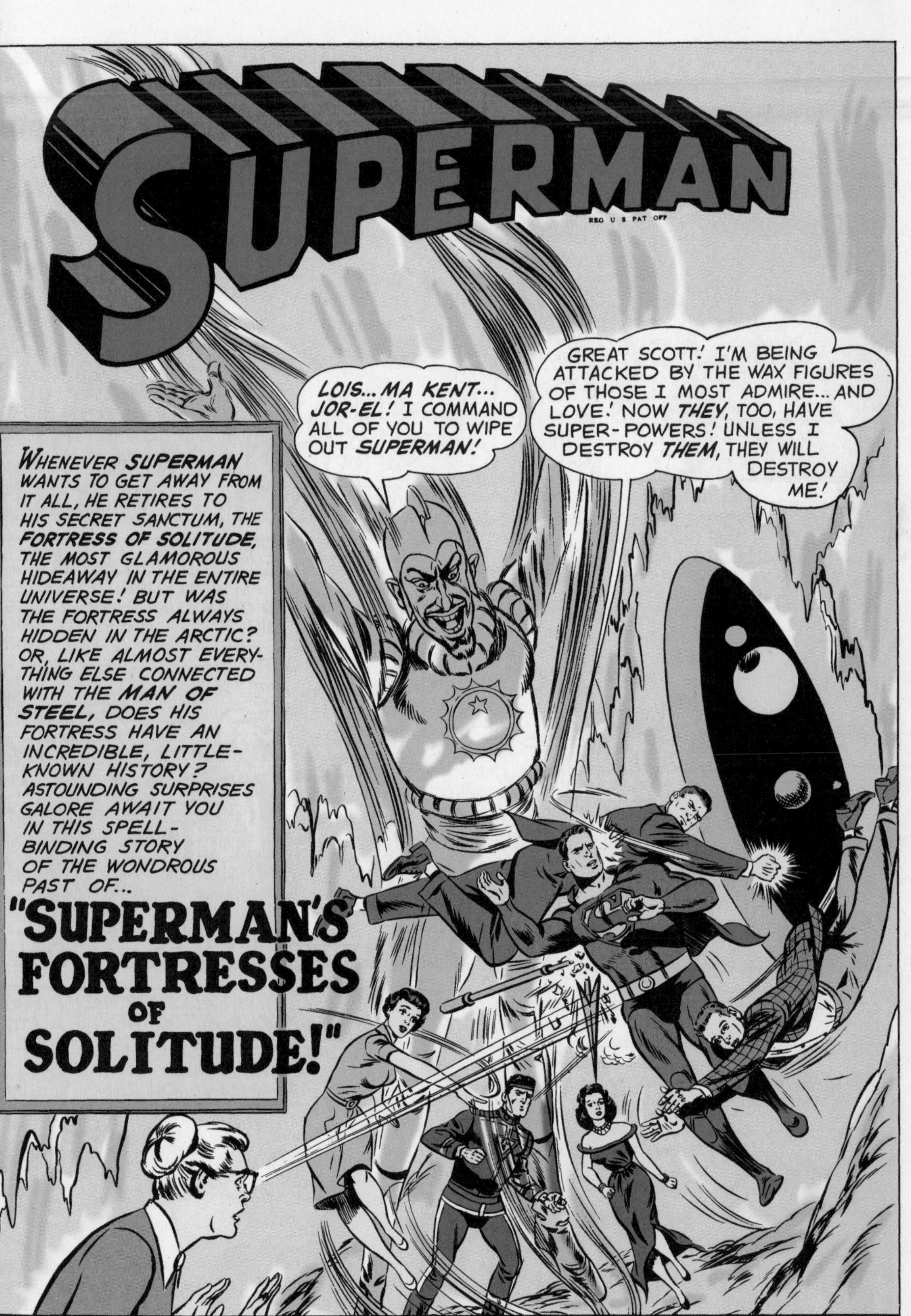
SUPERMAN
REG U S PAT OFF
WHENEVER SUPERMAN WANTS TO GET AWAY FROM IT ALL, HE RETIRES TO HIS SECRET SANCTUM, THE FORTRESS OF SOLITUDE, THE MOST GLAMOROUS HIDEAWAY IN THE ENTIRE UNIVERSE! BUT WAS THE FORTRESS ALWAYS HIDDEN IN THE ARCTIC? OR, LIKE ALMOST EVERYTHING ELSE CONNECTED WITH THE MAN OF STEEL, DOES HIS FORTRESS HAVE AN INCREDIBLE, LITTLE-KNOWN HISTORY? ASTOUNDING SURPRISES GALORE AWAIT YOU IN THIS SPELL-BINDING STORY OF THE WONDROUS PAST OF...
"SUPERMAN'S FORTRESSES OF SOLITUDE!"
LOIS... MA KENT... JOR-EL! I COMMAND ALL OF YOU TO WIPE OUT SUPERMAN!
GREAT SCOTT! I'M BEING ATTACKED BY THE WAX FIGURES OF THOSE I MOST ADMIRE... AND LOVE! NOW THEY, TOO, HAVE SUPER-POWERS! UNLESS I DESTROY THEM, THEY WILL DESTROY ME!

ONE AMAZING DAY, ON THE OUTSKIRTS OF METROPOLIS...
STEP RI-I-GHT THIS WAY, FOLKS! SEE THE ONE, THE ASTONISHING, SUPERMAN FORTRESS OF SOLITUDE!
GEE, MA! IS THIS REALLY SUPERMAN'S SECRET FORTRESS?
YES, ALVIN! SUPERMAN BROUGHT IT HERE FROM ITS SECRET LOCATION! HE IS PERSONALLY GUIDING PUBLIC TOURS THROUGH IT... AND ALL THE PROFITS WILL GO TO CHARITY!
WHY ARE THOSE TWO SUPERMAN ROBOTS ON GUAR
YOU MAY PASS!
SUPERMAN HAS MANY ENEMIES IN THE UNDERWORLD, AND THE ROBOTS ARE SCREENING ALL VISITORS WITH X-RAY VISION, TO MAKE SURE NOTHING DANGEROUS IS SMUGGLED IN WHICH CAN DAMAGE HIS FORTRESS!
ONE OF THE VISITORS MAKES A REQUEST...
SUPERMAN, I'M A WELDER, AND I COULD ONLY COME DURING MY LUNCH HOUR! IS IT OKAY IF I EAT DURING THE TOUR?
IT'S QUITE A RIGHT! JUST RELAX, AND ENJOY YOURSE
CHUCKLE! IMAGINE ME, TALKING TO THE MIGHTY SUPERMAN HIMSELF! WOULD YOU LIKE SOME COFFEE?
NO, BUT THANKS, ANYWAY!
TO THE HALL OF INTERPLANETARY MONSTER
2
ANOTHER VISITOR ASKS FOR THE MAN OF STEEL'S AUTOGRAPH...
I'M "BIG BOB" KRUGER, THE OIL MAN! HOW ABOUT YOUR AUTOGRAPH, SUPERMAN! YOU CAN USE MY PEN! BE SURE TO GIVE IT BACK, HA, HA!
HAPP TO OBLIG

RACIOUSLY, SUPERMAN LEADS AWED SITORS THROUGH THE FORTRESS...
OLKS! DO NOT BE FRIGHTENED BY NYTHING YOU SEE HERE! EVERY PRE- AUTION HAS BEEN TAKEN TO PROTECT VISITORS!
WH- WHO'S F-F-FRIGHTENED?

GASP! IT'S... BEAUTIFUL!...?? WHAT IS IT?
A RECENTLY ACQUIRED RAINBOW JEWEL FROM ANOTHER PLANET! ITS RADIATIONS HAVE A HEALTHFUL, INVIGORATING EFFECT UPON THE BEHOLDER! AND NOW, WOULD YOU LIKE TO SEE A KRYPTONIAN CITY?

RYPTONIAN CITY?!...EVERYBODY OWS THAT THE PLANET RYPTON BLEW UP SECONDS TER YOU LEFT IT IN A ROCKET, HEN YOU WERE A ABY!
THE CITY IS RIGHT HERE IN THIS BOTTLE, WHERE IT WAS PLACED BY THE SPACE-VILLAIN WHO REDUCED IT IN SIZE! YOU MAY LOOK AT IT THROUGH THE MAGNIFYING GLASS IF YOU WISH!

GEE! IT'S A REAL CITY, IN MINIATURE!
LET ME LOOK, TOO, KID!

HAT THE VISITORS SEE...

NEXT...
FOLKS, I CALL THIS STRANGE CREATURE FROM ANOTHER SOLAR SYSTEM THE WOTSIS! IT ATTACKS BY COMPRESSING ITSELF INTO A BALL, THEN FIRING ITSELF AT ITS OPPONENT LIKE A LIVING CANNON BALL! THE SPIKES ARE MADE OF STEEL!
WHAM!

AND THEN...
IN THIS ROOM, I HAVE RECREATED A 3-DIMENSIONAL TABLEAU OF THE EXACT MOMENT THAT THE PLANET KRYPTON EXPLODED! THE ROCKET REPRESENTS THE ONE IN WHICH I WAS SENT TO EARTH, AS A TINY SUPER-INFANT!

THE ASTOUNDING TOUR CONTINUES...
WHY ARE THESE DOORS LOCKED?
SOME OF THE ROOMS CONTAIN SUPER-SECRE WHICH NO OTHER PERSO MUST EVER LEARN! THE ARE FORBIDDEN TO ALL VISITORS!
KEEP OUT

SUDDENLY...
WHAT'S THAT NOISE AT THE FORTRESS' ENTRANCE?
ONE OF MY ROBOTS HAS SOUNDED AN ALARM! I'LL FIND OUT WHY!
R-R-R-R-RING!

GIVE ME BACK MY BOOK!
I SEE! MY ROBOT DETECTE A TINY TRANSMITTER, EMITTING A SUPER-SONIC SIGNAL, HIDDEN INSIDE THE HOLLOWED-OUT BOOK! TH HOOD PLANNED TO HIDE TH BOOK IN THE FORTRESS!
ZIP! ZIP!

WHEN I RETURN THE FORTRESS TO ITS SECRET LOCATION, CRIMINALS COULD HAVE TRACED IT WITH THE HELP OF THIS GADGET! TURN HIM OVER TO THE LAW, ROBOT Y!
YES, MASTER!... I WILL RETURN PROMPTLY!

ONCE AGAIN, SUPERMAN CONDUCTS THE TOUR... BUT TWO MEN TRAIL BEHIND THE OTHERS...THE "WELDER" AND THE "OIL MAN"...
NOW?
YEAH, NOW! LET'S DO IT, QUICK!

IFTLY, "BIG BOB" POURS THE INK FROM HIS FOUNTAIN
N INTO THE OTHER MAN'S THERMOS BOTTLE...
THIS WON'T SWEETEN YOUR COFFEE...
BUT IT WILL SURE KNOCK THE STUFFING OUT OF SUPERMAN'S FORTRESS OF SOLITUDE!
HA! HA!
AS THE "INK" COMBINES WITH THE "COFFEE", A DEADLY GAS FORMS...
L HIDE THE THERMOS
TTLE HERE! IF IT'S
UND TOO SOON, I CAN
Y I ACCIDENTALLY
RGOT IT!
CHUCKLE! THE ROBOTS DIDN'T DETECT WHAT WE WERE UP TO, BECAUSE THE CHEMICALS IN THE INK AND IN THE COFFEE WERE INDIVIDUALLY HARMLESS...
...BUT COMBINED, THE CHEMICALS FORM A GAS, WHICH WILL ERUPT INTO AN ATOMIC BLAST ONE HOUR FROM NOW!
JUST THE WAY OUR BOSS, THE CHIEF OF THE ANTI-SUPERMAN GANG, PLANNED!
KNOWN TO THE SCHEMERS, THEY ARE BEING
SERVED BY SCIENTISTS IN KANDOR CITY, THE
Y CITY IN THE BOTTLE RESTING ON A
RTRESS NICHE...
GASP! THEY'RE PLOTTING AGAINST THE FORTRESS!
WARN SUPERMAN!
I CAN'T GET THROUGH! OUR SUPER-SONIC SIGNAL IS JUST A JUMBLE OF STATIC!
IMPOSSIBLE!

I'VE DISCOVERED THE CAUSE OF THE STATIC! IT'S THE RAINBOW JEWEL! IT HAS SET UP INTERFERENCE TO OUR SUPER-SONIC SIGNAL! WE CAN'T PIERCE THAT INTERFERENCE!
KEEP TRYING!

NOT ONLY THE FORTRESS... BUT THE FATE OF OUR CITY, A
EVERY SOUL IN IT...DEPENDS
OUR GETTING THE WARNING THROUGH TO SUPERMAN!

MEANWHILE...SUPERMAN IS UNAWARE OF THE MENACE THAT THREATENS THE FORTRESS AND KANDOR CITY...
WHAT AN EVIL FACE! WHAT'S THE STORY BEHIND THAT TROPHY, SUPERMAN?
SORRY, BUT I PREFER TO KEEP IT CONFIDENTIAL!
URKO THE TERRIBLE

THESE VISITORS WOULD BE ASTOUNDED, IF THEY KNEW T
STORY! I REMEMBER IT ALL CLEARLY, AS THOUGH IT HAD HAPPENED ONLY YESTERDA

HIS THOUGHTS WINGING BACK, SUPERMAN RECALLS THE TIME HIS FORTRESS HAD EXISTED IN OUTER SPACE, DISGUISED AS A METEOR...
NOTHING CAN BEAT THIS, FOR PRIVACY!

THEN, ONE DAY, INSIDE THE METEOR FORTRESS...
THAT STRANGE SPACE-CLOUD APPROACHING! IT MAY BE MY IMAGINATION...BUT...IT SEEMS ALIVE...AND...MENACING...

ND AS THE SPACE-CLOUD HAD ENGULFED THE ATELLITE OF SOLITUDE...
OME OF THE CLOUD AS PENETRATED THE IP, DEFYING SCIENCE! ..FEEL A SENSE OF...DREAD .AS THOUGH SOMETHING... ERRIBLE... IS ABOUT TO APPEN! IS IT...JUST A ASE OF.. NERVES?

NO, SUPERMAN... IT IS NOT NERVES! I AM URKO THE TERRIBLE, A CLOUD-INTELLIGENCE! I HATE ALL OTHER FORMS OF LIFE... INCLUDING YOU!
YOU'RE...EVIL! GET OUT! GREAT GUNS! YOU'RE AS HARD TO GRASP AS SMOKE!

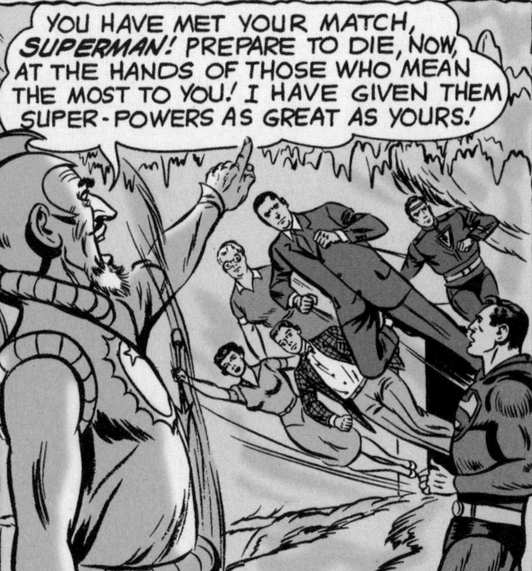
YOU HAVE MET YOUR MATCH, SUPERMAN! PREPARE TO DIE, NOW, AT THE HANDS OF THOSE WHO MEAN THE MOST TO YOU! I HAVE GIVEN THEM SUPER-POWERS AS GREAT AS YOURS!

GOOD GRIEF! URKO HAS CAUSED THE WAX DUMMIES IN MY TROPHY ROOM TO COME TO LIFE!

DEATH TO SUPERMAN!
DESTROY HIM!
WIPE HIM OUT!
BRAVO, URKO!
I KNOW THEY'RE ONLY SUPER-DUMMIES, ANIMATED BY THE SPACE-CLOUD'S EVIL INTELLIGENCE...BUT I HAVEN'T THE HEART TO FIGHT EVEN THE DUMMIES OF LOIS...JIMMY...PERRY... MA AND PA KENT...JOR-EL AND LARA!
7

BAH! HE'S TOO INVULNERABLE! NEVER MIND HIM! DESTROY EARTH, MY PETS! BUT WAIT AN HOUR FIRST!
WHY SHOULD THEY WAIT AN HOUR BEFORE ATTACKING EARTH?

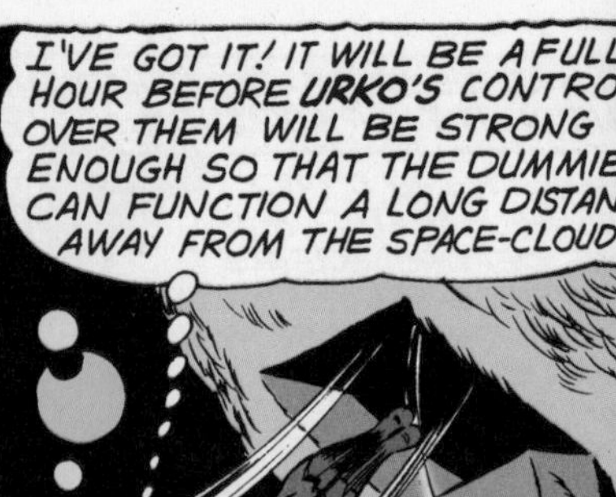
I'VE GOT IT! IT WILL BE A FULL HOUR BEFORE URKO'S CONTRO OVER THEM WILL BE STRONG ENOUGH SO THAT THE DUMMIE CAN FUNCTION A LONG DISTAN AWAY FROM THE SPACE-CLOUD

DELIBERATELY, SUPERMAN PROPELLED A GIANT FLAMING SUN TOWARD THE SPACE-CLOUD, WITH MIGHTY GUSTS OF HIS SUPER-BREATH...
IT'S TRYING TO FLEE! NOW IT'S MY TURN TO TURN ON THE HEAT!

EEE-URRR-OWWWWW!
THE SUN IS CONSUMIN THE SPACE-CLOUD! TH DUMMIES WILL BECOM LIFELESS AGAIN, WITH URKO DESTROYED! HMM...THIS EPISODE TEACHES ME A LESSON! I'LL NEVER AGAIN KEEP FORTRESS IN SPACE! I CAN RISK RUNNING INTO OTHE UNKNOWN SPACE DANGERS!

AND AS SUPERMAN'S RECOLLECTION ENDS...HOPE IN THE TINY KRYPTON CITY FADES...
YOU MUST KEEP TRYING!
NO USE...THE RAINBOW JEWEL'S STATIC-CREATING INTERFERENCE...HAS DOOMED US...
8

... WHILE THE CRIMINALS EXULT...
C'MON! WE'D BETTER JOIN THE OTHERS!
NOT YET! A JOB AS CLEVER AS THIS DESERVE TO BE GLOATED OVER! HA! AND SUPERMAN THINKS THERE'S COFFEE IN THIS THERMOS BOTTLE

MEANWHILE...
HAT AN ODD CREATURE! TINY FLAME-MAN! IS ALIVE, SUPERMAN?
NO, I FASHIONED IT IN MEMORY OF AN ADVENTURE THAT HAPPENED LONG AGO! SORRY... I DON'T WANT TO TELL THE STORY BEHIND THIS TROPHY, EITHER!
YES, SUPERMAN WON'T TALK...BUT HIS MEMORY RECREATES THE TIME HE HAD TRANSPORTED HIS FORTRESS OF SOLITUDE INTO THE CENTER OF THE EARTH...
SURELY, I'LL FIND PEACE AND QUIET, HERE! AND THIS LOCATION FOR MY FORTRESS SHOULD BE SAFER THAN OUTER SPACE!
UESS AGAIN, SUPERMAN!
GOOD GRIEF! I'M ATTACKED BY FIRE-PEOPLE! B-BUT WHY? I HAVE NO INTENTION OF HARMING THEM!
AND THEN, THE MAN OF STEEL HAD PICKED UP HIS WEIRD ATTACKERS' TELEPATHIC SHOUTS...
DESTROY THE MONSTER!
GOOD GOSH! THEY THINK THE FORTRESS IS AN INVADING VESSEL, AND THAT I AM A MONSTER COME TO HARM THEM! THEY HAVE PANICKED, JUST THE WAY SOME SURFACE WORLD PEOPLE WOULD SCARE IF A SPACE-SHIP LANDED AND A STRANGE BEING GOT OUT!
THE FIRE-BOMBS OPENED A FISSURE AND AN UNDERGROUND STREAM IS GUSHING THROUGH! WATER IS THE FIRE-PEOPLE'S GREATEST ENEMY!
FLEE!
WE'LL ALL DIE! IT'S HOPELESS!
9

ACTING SWIFTLY, SUPERMAN HAD HOLLOWED OUT A GREAT CREVICE...
HE DIVERTED THE WATER AWAY FROM US! THE MONSTER SAVED OUR LIVES!
HE IS NO MONSTER! HE IS... A FRIEND...
NO! DON'T GO, MONSTER...I MEAN, FRIEND! WE MADE A MISTAKE, AND WE ARE SORRY! STAY!!
SO LONG, FOLKS! I DON'T MIND YOUR FIERY TEMPERS... IT'S JUST THAT THE CENTER OF THE EARTH ISN'T AS PEACEFUL AS I THOUGHT IT WOULD BE!
BACK IN THE PRESENT, AS SUPERMA
ENEMIES BECOME ANXIOUS...
YOU'VE GLOATED ENOUGH! IF WE DON'T REJOIN THE OTHERS RIGHT AWAY, OUR ABSENCE MAY BE NOTICED!
OKAY! OKAY!
SOON, AFTER THE CRIMINALS REJOIN THE OTHER VISITORS...
THAT FINISHES THE TOUR, FOLKS! GLAD YOU CAME!
YOU WON'T BE SO GLAD AFTER YOUR PRECIOUS FORTRESS BLOWS TO SMITHEREENS!
10
AND IN THE TINY CITY WITHIN THE BOTTLE...
WE MUST TRY AGAIN TO CONTACT SUPERMAN!
NO USE TRYING! TH
STATIC FROM THE
RAINBOW JEWE
HAS RUINED OUR ON
CHANCE! ONLY A LEA
BARRIER CAN BLOC
ITS RADIATIONS!

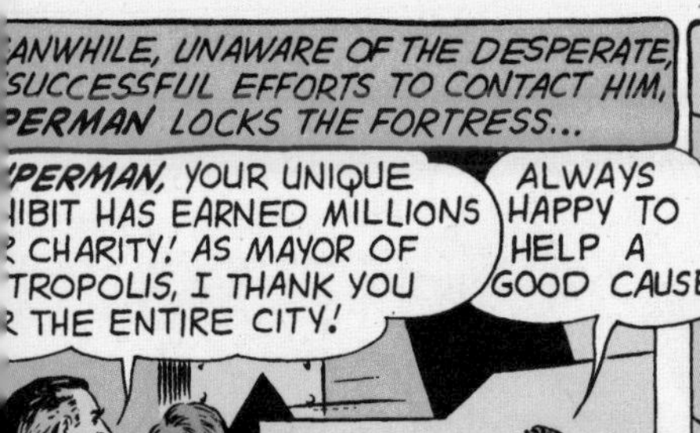
ANWHILE, UNAWARE OF THE DESPERATE,
SUCCESSFUL EFFORTS TO CONTACT HIM,
PERMAN LOCKS THE FORTRESS...
PERMAN, YOUR UNIQUE
IBIT HAS EARNED MILLIONS
CHARITY! AS MAYOR OF
TROPOLIS, I THANK YOU
THE ENTIRE CITY!
ALWAYS
HAPPY TO
HELP A
GOOD CAUSE!

CLICK!

BACK TO THE ARCTIC FLIES THE
MAN OF STEEL...
NOTHING
LIKE A JOB
WELL DONE!

ANWHILE, AT THE ANTI-SUPERMAN
NG HIDEOUT...
TCH THE SEISMOGRAPH NEEDLE, BOYS!
HEN THE NEEDLE JUMPS, IT WILL MEAN
ERE'S BEEN AN ATOMIC EXPLOSION THAT
S WIPED OUT SUPERMAN'S BELOVED
RTRESS! IT WILL TAKE HIM YEARS TO
REPLACE IT!

EYES GLEAMING LIKE PREDATORY BEASTS, THE
GANGLEADER AND HIS MEN WAIT BREATHLESSLY...
THIS SUSPENSE...
IS MURDER!
SHUT UP, AND
WATCH THAT NEEDLE!

OM OVERHANGS KANDOR CITY!
ET'S TRY
AIN, MARS-OL!
IT'S USELESS, RA-HO,
BUT... ALL RIGHT...

A FEW MOMENTS LATER...
LOOK AT THAT
NEEDLE JUMP!
WOW!!
I DID IT! I DID
IT!!... I'VE DESTROYED
SUPERMAN'S FORTRESS
OF SOLITUDE! HA! HA HA!
I WISH I COULD LAUGH IN
HIS INVULNERABLE FACE
RIGHT NOW!

GREETINGS, CLODS!
SUPERMAN! YOU'VE CAUGHT US! WELL, I DON'T CARE, AS LONG AS WE SUCCEEDED IN DESTROYING YOUR FORTRESS! HA! HA!

THE LAUGH IS ON YOU! YOU DIDN'T WRECK THE FORTRESS, AFTER ALL!
YOU'RE LYING! THE SEISMOGRAPH NEEDLE SHOWED THAT AN ATOM EXPLOSION OCCURRED THE EXACT SECOND PLANNED!

THERE WAS AN ATOMIC EXPLOSION, ALL RIGHT! BUT IT OCCURRED AFTER I HURLED THE THERMOS BOTTLE TO WHERE AN EXPLOSION COULDN'T HARM THE FORTRESS!
GROAN H-HOW DID YOU FIND OUT ABOUT OUR PLOT?

THAT'S MY SECRET!... ENJOY YOUR PRISON SENTENCE!

LATER... IN HIS FORTRESS, SUPERMAN COMMUNICATES WITH KANDOR CITY'S SCIENTISTS...
HOW FORTUNATE THAT YOU DID NOT GIVE UP YOUR DESPERATE ATTEMPT TO CONTACT ME! AFTER I REPLACED THE FORTRESS IN ITS ORIGINAL HIDING PLACE, I ENTERED AND NOTICED THAT A LEAD THERMOS BOTTLE CAP COVERED THE RAIN-BOW JEWEL...
IT HAD BEEN DISCARDED BY ONE OF THE CROOKS! IRONICALLY, IT FELL OVER THE RAINBOW JEWEL! ITS LEAD STRUCTURE CUT OFF THE INTERFERING STATIC CAUSED BY THE JEWEL'S RADIATIONS!
BECAUSE OF THE CRIMINAL'S CARELESSNESS, WE WERE FINALLY ABLE TO GET THROUGH TO YOU, WARN YOU OF THE PLOT IN TIME, AND DIRECT YOU TO THE SCHEMERS' HEADQUARTERS!
BE ASSURE I WILL DESTR THE RAINBO JEWEL SO THAT IT WILL NEVER PREVEN CONTACT BETWE US AGAIN!
The End.

DC
$2.50
SUPERMAN
AND HIS INCREDIBLE
FORTRESS OF SOLITUDE
ALL-NEW
COLLECTOR'S
EDITION!

THE MAGAZINE THAT YOU DEMANDED!
LEARN ALL THE ASTONISHING SECRETS OF SUPERMAN'S SPECTACULAR SANCTUARY!

ROCKETED AS A BABY FROM THE EXPLODING PLANET KRYPTON, KAL-EL CAME TO EARTH--WHOSE ENVIRONMENT GAVE HIM FANTASTIC POWERS! IN METROPOLIS, HE POSES AS CLARK KENT--BUT BATTLES EVIL THE WORLD OVER AS...
SUPERMAN®
Created by JERRY SIEGEL & JOE SHUSTER
METROPOLIS! ONE OF THE LARGEST CITIES IN THE UNITED STATES--IN THE WORLD! IT ALWAYS CHOKES ME UP JUST TO VIEW IT FROM 'WAY UP HERE'!
BUT IF I DON'T GET A MOVE ON, THERE'LL BE NOTHING LEFT OF IT IN A FEW MINUTES--NOTHING BUT A CRATER ROUGHLY THE SIZE OF RHODE ISLAND!
YET TODAY, THE MAN OF STEEL FACES THE GREATEST CHALLENGE OF HIS LONG AND TRIUMPH-STUDDED CAREER, AS HE CONFRONTS A WORLD-SHATTERING TRAGEDY WHOSE ULTIMATE ARCHITECT MAY HAVE BEEN --HIMSELF!
FORTRESS OF FEAR!
SSSSS
ROY THOMAS WRITER
ROSS ANDRU AND ROMEO TANGHAL ARTISTS
LETTERER-GASPAR
COLORIST-J. SERPE
LEN WEIN EDITORIAL SERVICES INC
FEATURING THE THOUSAND-AND-ONE STARTLING SECRETS OF THE FORTRESS OF SOLITUDE!
1

Hmmm... FUNNY THE THINGS THAT CROSS YOUR MIND, EVEN IN MOMENTS OF CRISIS!
RIGHT NOW, FOR INSTANCE, I KEEP REMEMBERING THAT "BATTLE-CRY" THE MEDIA PEOPLE MADE UP FOR ME--BUT WHICH I NEVER REALLY SAID, TILL THEY TOLD ME ABOUT IT.
COME TO THINK OF IT, THOUGH-- THIS IS ONE TIME IT ACTUALLY FITS, SO--
UP--
UP--
--AND AWAY!
2

AWAY FROM EARTH, THAT IS--
--EVEN IF IT'S ONLY FOR A FEW SHORT SECONDS, AND FOR A MISSION THAT SHOULD BE DUCK SOUP FOR ME TO PERFORM!
STRANGE! I'LL PROBABLY BE BACK IN THE DAILY PLANET BUILDING EVEN BEFORE I'M MISSED, WITHOUT EVEN WORKING UP MUCH OF A SWEAT.
YET, IF I WEREN'T AROUND, METROPOLIS' TEEMING MILLIONS WOULD BE DOOMED--
--AND THE RESULTANT EARTHQUAKES AND TIDAL WAVES MIGHT EASILY KILL AND MAIM MORE PEOPLE THAN ALL OF WORLD WAR TWO!
3

YET, IT ALL BEGAN SO QUIETLY, ONLY A FEW MINUTES AGO--
--WITH FOUR PEOPLE SITTING AROUND A TV SCREEN WATCHING A SHOW DEDICATED TO--
--PEACE! YES, LADIES AND GENTLEMEN, THAT IS THE VERY SPECIAL THEME OF TODAY'S VERY SPECIAL MEETING OF THE UNITED NATION'S GENERAL ASSEMBLY HERE IN NEW YORK CITY...!
AMAZING, ISN'T IT, PERRY A FEW DECADES AGO, TELEVISION WAS ONLY AN AMUSING NOVELTY--
BUT TODAY'S TELE-CAST IS GOING OUT LIVE TO AN ESTIMATED ONE BILLION PEOPLE!
THEN LET'S HOPE IT PROMOTES SOME OF THAT PEACE SHE'S TALKING ABOUT!
LORD KNOWS, THE WORLD COULD USE SOME, RIGHT ABOUT NOW!
AND NOW, WE TAKE YOU INSIDE TO-- SQUAWWKK!
HEY! WHAT--?
SOMETHING'S HAPPENING TO THE PICTURE--
--AND, ASTONISHINGLY, NOT JUST IN THIS SET--BUT IN TV SETS ALL OVER THE CITY--
--CAN'T TELL PERRY, LOIS, AND JIMMY I CAN SEE THAT, OF COURSE!
CONFOUND THESE NEW-FANGLED--!
UH, I'M SURE IT'S JUST SOME MOMENTARY INTER-FERENCE WITH THE SATELLITE SIGNAL, PERRY!
OH YEAH? SINCE WHEN DID YOU BECOME A TV REPAIRMAN, KENT? I--
HEY, CHIEF-- LOOK!
TH-THERE'S A NEW IMAGE FORMING!
AND IT'S DEFINITELY NOT BARBARA WALTERS!
GOOD AFTERNOON, MEN AND WOMEN OF EARTH!
ALLOW ME TO INTRODUCE MYSELF.
YOU MAY CALL ME-- DOMINUS!
UH OH! WHY AM I SO SURE THIS GUY SPELLS TROUBLE!?
4

BECAUSE I HAVE PATCHED INTO THE U.S.A.'S TELECOMMUNICATION'S NETWORK, MY WORDS ARE BEING BEAMED TO THE LARGEST AUDIENCE IN HISTORY-- WHICH IS ONLY FITTING.
FOR, EVERY MAN, WOMAN, AND CHILD ON EARTH WILL BE AFFECTED BY WHAT I AM ABOUT TO SAY-- AND BY WHAT I HAVE ALREADY DONE--!
INCREDIBLE! HE'S MANAGED SOMEHOW TO ACHIEVE INSTANTANEOUS TRANSLATION OF HIS WORDS INTO LITERALLY HUNDREDS OF LANGUAGES--
--SO THAT UNTOLD MILLIONS WILL BE ABLE NOT ONLY TO HEAR--BUT TO UNDERSTAND!
AND WHAT HAVE I DONE, YOU MAY ASK?..
WHY, SIMPLY THIS:
BY ELECTRO-MAGNETIC MEANS, I HAVE PULLED A COLOSSAL METEOR IN FROM DEEP SPACE-- AND GREATLY ACCELERATED ITS VELOCITY.
THUS, EVEN AS YOUR ASTRONOMERS ARE ONLY FIRST OBSERVING IT-- IT IS ONLY MINUTES AWAY FROM STRIKING THE EASTERN COAST OF THE UNITED STATES!
G-GOOD LORD!
EXCUSE ME! I--I THINK I'M GOING TO BE SICK!
WHAT I WAS REALLY GOING TO BE, OF COURSE-- WAS SUPERMAN!!
EVEN THOSE WHO MIGHT REJOICE AT A DISASTER BEFALLING AMERICA WOULD SOON THINK TWICE--WHEN THE AFTERMATH OF THE METEORITE'S IMPACT MIGHT MAKE THE VERY ATMOSPHERE OF THE ENTIRE EARTH UNINHABITABLE!
WELL, THERE IT IS--
--AND THE MYSTERIOUS "DOMINUS" SURE WASN'T KIDDING ABOUT ITS SIZE AND MASS!
STILL, MY X-RAY VISION DOESN'T DETECT ANY KRYPTONITE IN ITS MAKEUP...
5

SO, NO MATTER HOW BIG--OR HOW DENSE--I SHOULD STILL BE ABLE TO TOTAL IT BY HITTING IT FULL-OUT!
EITHER THAT, OR IT'LL TOTAL ME--AND EARTH CAN START LOOKING FOR A NEW CHAMPION OF TRUTH, JUSTICE, AND THE AMERICAN WAY!
WELL, NOBODY EVER PROMISED ME I WAS GOING TO LIVE FOREVER!
HERE GOES THE PROVERBIAL NOTHING!
YET, THE SCION OF STEEL IS NOT UNRUFFLED BY WHAT FOLLOWS...
HUH?? WHAT'S CAUSING THESE SHOCK WAVES--WHEN THAT HUNK OF ROCK HAD VIRTUALLY NO ATMOSPHERE?
AND WHY SHOULD THEY BOWL ME OVER LIKE A COSTUMED TENPIN?
BUT--WAIT A MINUTE! THAT'S NOT ALL!--
THE EARTH I JUST SAVED-IT LOOKS--DIFFERENT, SOMEHOW! CAN'T--QUITE
THE EARTH'S LAND-MASSES ARE WHERE THEY SHOULD BE--EXACTLY ONE HOUR FROM NOW!
6

THE RESULT OF THE COLLISION-IN-SPACE OF THESE TWO SEEMINGLY ALL-BUT-IRRESISTABLE FORCES, HOWEVER, IS FAR FROM NOTHING.
RATHER, THE AWESOME OUTCOME IS TRULY SOMETHING--
--NAMELY, A MIND-STAGGERING EXPLOSION HERE IN THE SOUNDLESS REACHES BEYOND EARTH'S STRATOSPHERE, AS MAN MEETS METEOR HEAD-ON!
AND IT IS THE MAN WHO WINS--
--BECAUSE HE IS SUPERMAN!
YES! NOW I SEE! THE POSITION OF THE CONTINENTS--IN RELATION TO WHERE THEY WERE JUST AN INSTANT BEFORE I STRUCK THE METEOR--
BUT, SINCE THAT'S IMPOSSIBLE--THEN IT MUST BE THAT THE SHOCK OF COLLISION KNOCKED ME EVER SO SLIGHTLY INTO THE FUTURE, SOMEHOW--SO THAT I'M SEEING THE EARTH AS IT WILL BE, PRECISELY ONE HOUR FROM--
GREAT KRYPTON! NOW WHAT??
THAT SUDDEN FLASH OF LIGHT--LIKE ANOTHER EXPLOSION--NEAR THE NORTH POLE--!
IT'S CAUSING TERRIFIC REVERBERATIONS--GREAT CRACKS IN THE VERY EARTH ITSELF!
I KNOW THOSE SIGNS! TH-THE EARTH IS ABOUT TO--
7

I'D BETTER CHECK THE EARTH'S CORE, JUST TO MAKE SURE THAT--NOPE! NOTHING WRONG THERE!

NO FANTASTIC PRES-SURES BUILDING UP THERE--SUCH AS CAUSED KRYPTON'S DEATH, WHEN I WAS AN INFANT!

BUT THAT DOESN'T EXACTLY GET ME OFF THE HOOK--

FOR AN INSTANT--A FEW SECONDS AT MOST--I WAS AN UNWILLING WITNESS TO THE FUTURE--

--AND IT WAS DEADLY-- FOR MORE THAN FOUR BILLION PEOPLE!

--BECAUSE I SAW THE EXACT SPOT WHERE THAT EARTH-EXPLOSION BEGAN-- OR WILL BEGIN, IF I WASN'T SEEING THINGS--

--AND IT WAS TOO PINPOINT-PERFECT TO BE A MERE COINCIDENCE!

GOT TO GET BACK TO EARTH FAST-- FASTER THAN I'VE EVER MOVED BEFORE!

YES, THAT'S IT, SUPERMAN! SWOOP EARTHWARD AT THE SPEED OF SOUND--OF LIGHT-- NAY, OF TIME ITSELF!

IN THE END, IT WILL AVAIL YOU NOTHING!

THE EARTH IS DOOMED!!

8

THEN SUPERMAN DID GET A GLIMPSE OF THE FUTURE, DOMINUS-- JUST LIKE YOU WANTED HIM TO!?
OF COURSE, MY DEAR ROGER! I DO NOT MAKE ERRORS IN CALCULATION.
FROM THE MOMENT I LEARNED OF THAT METEOR'S EXISTENCE, I KNEW FROM SPECTRO-ANALYSIS--
--THAT A COLLISION BETWEEN IT AND SUPERMAN'S KRYPTONIAN FRAME WOULD RESULT IN HIS BEING HURLED PRECISELY ONE HOUR INTO THE FUTURE!
YEAH--BUT IT WAS JUST FOR A COUPLE'A SECONDS!
HOW LONG DOES IT TAKE, FOOL, FOR ONE TO SEE THE DREAMS OF A LIFETIME GO UP IN FIRE AND SMOKE?
A FEW SECONDS WAS QUITE LONG ENOUGH TO MAKE THE MAN OF STEEL STRIVE MIGHTILY FOR THE NEXT SIXTY MINUTES TO PREVENT THAT HORRIFIC FUTURE!
LONG ENOUGH FOR HIM TO SUFFER--
--AND LONG ENOUGH, I AM CERTAIN--FOR HIM TO FAIL!
AS, AMID THE FREEZING COLD OF EARTH'S ARCTIC REGIONS...
THERE IT IS--THE VERY SPOT WHERE, IF MY VISION HOLDS TRUE, AN EXPLOSION WILL BEGIN THAT WILL TEAR THE WHOLE PLANET ASUNDER, LESS THAN AN HOUR FROM NOW!
FROM ABOVE--OR EVEN FROM BELOW--NO MORTAL EYE WOULD SEE ANYTHING BUT A MASSIVE MOUNTAIN OF ICE.
BUT MY X-RAY VISION REVEALS THAT PART OF THE FACE OF THAT MOUNTAIN IS MERELY AN ILLUSION, MASKING A HUGE DOOR--
--THE SECRET ENTRANCE-WAY TO MY OWN FORTRESS OF SOLITUDE!
9

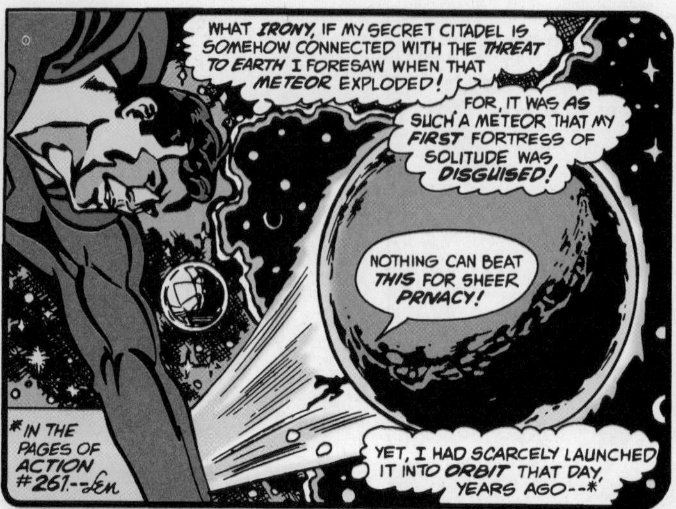
WHAT IRONY, IF MY SECRET CITADEL IS SOMEHOW CONNECTED WITH THE THREAT TO EARTH I FORESAW WHEN THAT METEOR EXPLODED!
FOR, IT WAS AS SUCH A METEOR THAT MY FIRST FORTRESS OF SOLITUDE WAS DISGUISED!
NOTHING CAN BEAT THIS FOR SHEER PRIVACY!
YET, I HAD SCARCELY LAUNCHED IT INTO ORBIT THAT DAY, YEARS AGO--*
*IN THE PAGES OF ACTION #261.--Len

"--WHEN SUDDENLY--"
WHAT--? SOME SORT OF SPACE-CLOUD APPROACHING--AND IT SEEMS--ALIVE!
YES, SUPERMAN! I AM URKO THE TERRIBLE--
--SWORN FOE OF ALL OTHER FORMS OF LIFE!

"THE MALEVOLENT INTELLIGENCE OF URKO NOT ONLY CAUSED THE WAX DUMMIES I HAD MADE OF MY EARTH-BORN FRIENDS TO COME TO LIFE--BUT ALSO ENDOWED THEM WITH SUPER-POWERS!..."
DEATH TO SUPERMAN!
DESTROY HIM!
"I WAS TOO INVULNERABLE TO DESTROY, HOWEVER--

"--SO THE LIVING SPACE-CLOUD TOOK ANOTHER TACK:
WE SHALL WAIT ONE HOUR MY PETS--AND THEN WE SHALL DESTROY THE EARTH, INSTEAD
WAIT AN HOUR!? URKO MUST NEED TIME TO COMPLETE HIS CONTROL OVER THE WAX IMAGES!
WELL, I'M NOT GOING TO GIVE IT TO HIM!

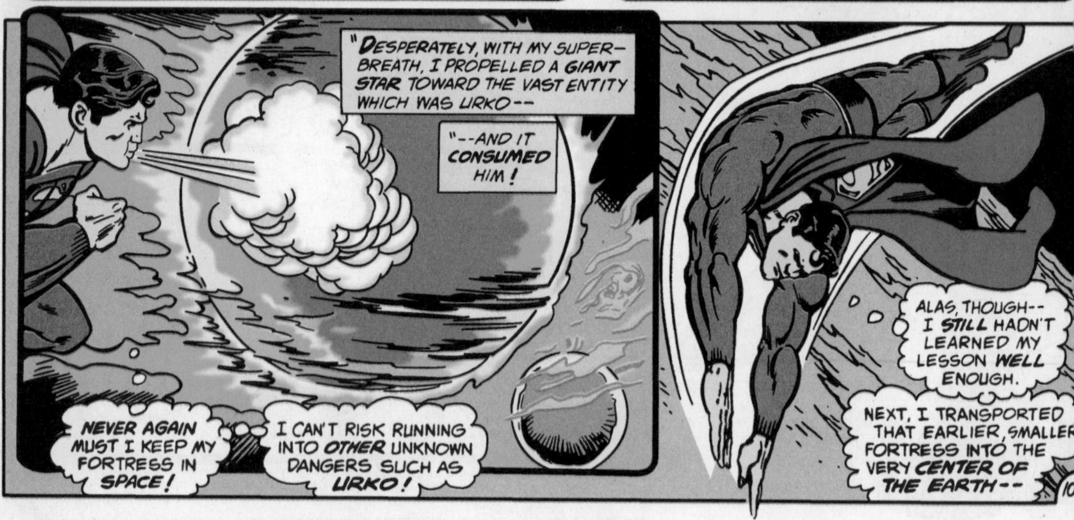
"DESPERATELY, WITH MY SUPER-BREATH, I PROPELLED A GIANT STAR TOWARD THE VAST ENTITY WHICH WAS URKO--
"--AND IT CONSUMED HIM!
NEVER AGAIN MUST I KEEP MY FORTRESS IN SPACE!
I CAN'T RISK RUNNING INTO OTHER UNKNOWN DANGERS SUCH AS URKO!
ALAS, THOUGH--I STILL HADN'T LEARNED MY LESSON WELL ENOUGH.
NEXT, I TRANSPORTED THAT EARLIER, SMALLER FORTRESS INTO THE VERY CENTER OF THE EARTH--
10

"I HAD HOPED TO FIND BOTH SAFETY AS WELL AS PEACE AND QUIET NEAR THE EARTH'S CORE, BUT INSTEAD--"
ATTACK! ATTACK!
DESTROY THE MONSTER!
GOOD GRIEF! I'M BEING ASSAULTED BY A RACE OF FIRE-PEOPLE!
THEY MUST THINK I'M SOME SORT OF INVADER COME TO HARM THEM.

"THEIR RECKLESSLY-HURLED FIRE-BOMBS, HOWEVER, HAD OPENED A FISSURE, THROUGH WHICH A GREAT UNDERGROUND RIVER RUSHED IN...
FLEE!
IT IS HOPELESS! WE SHALL ALL DIE!

"FORTUNATELY FOR THEM, I WAS ABLE TO HOLLOW OUT A GREAT CANAL AT SUPER-SPEED...

"...INTO WHICH THE RAGING SUBTERRANEAN CATARACT WAS DIVERTED."
THERE! THAT SHOULD END THE MENACE TO THAT RACE OF... uh... HOT-HEADS!

"THE FIRE-PEOPLE REALIZED THEY HAD ERRED, AND TRIED TO PERSUADE ME TO STAY, BUT--"

...THAT STRONGHOLD WHICH WAS TO BE MY SECRET SANCTUM... MY HIDEAWAY...
...THE ONE PLACE, PERHAPS, IN ALL THE UNIVERSE, WHERE I COULD COME TO STUDY... TO CONTEMPLATE... OR SIMPLY TO RELAX...
...TO SHUT OUT THE WHOLE WORLD, AND BE ALONE... AS EVERY MAN NEEDS TO BE, AT LEAST ONCE IN A WHILE!
RIGHT NOW, THOUGH, IT'S THE FORTRESS ITSELF THAT WILL GET MY UNDIVIDED ATTENTION!
I'LL JUST OPEN THE DOOR WITH THE GIANT KEY I'VE PLACED HERE, SO I CAN GO INSIDE AND START--
WAIT! WHY DO I ASSUME THAT THE MENACE TO EARTH MUST BE INSIDE THE FORTRESS?
WHY COULDN'T IT BE SOMETHING RIGHT OUTSIDE IT--LIKE THE KEY ITSELF?...
"I REMEMBER HOW, YEARS AGO, I FIRST DISCOVERED THIS DESOLATE SPOT--AND RETURNED LATER, TO TURN THAT DESOLATION TO MY ADVANTAGE..." *
THIS IS THE IDEAL SPOT FOR THE FORTRESS I HAVE IN MIND!
* SEE SUPERMAN #176. --LEN.
"USING MY BARE HANDS, I CARVED FROM SOLID ROCK THE REFUGE I YEARNED FOR...
THRAK
"...AS WELL AS THE MASSIVE KEY THERETO!"
NOBODY ELSE ON EARTH COULD UNLOCK THE PLACE, EVEN IF THEY STUMBLED ONTO IT!
BY DISGUISING THE KEY AS A HUGE AIRPLANE MARKER, INSTALLED ON A MOUNTAIN PEAK, IT WILL EVEN GUIDE PILOTS SAFELY THROUGH THIS ICY WILDERNESS.
12

FOR, THE ALMOST-INDISPUTABLE EVIDENCE IS THAT SOMETHING WITHIN IT WILL CAUSE A MIGHTY EXPLOSION LESS THAN AN HOUR FROM NOW--
--AN EXPLOSION THAT WILL MEAN THE END OF THE WORLD!
LATER, I CREATED A NEW METAL SO TOUGH THAT EVEN I COULD PENETRATE IT ONLY WITH THE HELP OF AN ULTRA-HARD DIAMOND.
"TO TEST THE METAL, I PLOPPED A MONOLITH MADE OF IT DOWN IN THE MIDDLE OF METROPOLIS PARK..."
WHAT THE HECK IS THIS THING--AND HOW'D IT GET HERE?
I DUNNO-- BUT THE MAYOR WANTS IT MOVED!
*ACTION #409. --Len.
"...WHERE IT RESISTED THE BEST EFFORTS OF A SPECIAL DEMOLITION SQUAD TO DESTROY, DAMAGE, OR EVEN DENT IT.
ACID
"ONLY CAPT. HORACE MITCHELL, IN CHARGE OF THAT SQUAD, KNEW I HAD SECRETLY PLACED IT THERE IN THE NIGHT...
"...AND NOT EVEN HE HAD ANY IDEA WHY!
13

"FROM THAT DAY TO THIS, NO ONE ELSE HAS EVER KNOWN IT WAS I WHO REMOVED THE MONOLITH, AS WELL.
"REACHING THE NORTH POLE, I SOON EMPLOYED MY SPECIAL DIAMOND DRILL TO CUT OUT A LARGE KEYHOLE...
"AND MY HANDS TO SMOOTH OUT SAME...
"...AND THAT WAS THAT!
I'VE ALSO EQUIPPED THE KEYHOLE WITH ENOUGH PROTECTIVE DEVICES THAT NO ONE COULD SLIP THROUGH IT, EVEN AT SUPER-SPEED...
...AT LEAST, NOT WITHOUT SETTING OFF AN ULTRASONIC ALARM WHICH ONLY I COULD HEAR, WHEREVER I WAS.*
SO, SINCE I DIDN'T HEAR THE ALARM, I CAN ASSUME NOBODY'S BEEN INSIDE THE FORTRESS SINCE I WAS.
*ACTION COMICS #407.--Len
THERE! I'LL HANG THE KEY HERE, TILL I LEAVE.
I USED TO HANG IT UP RIGHT BESIDE THE DOOR OUTSIDE AS WELL.
...BUT I DECIDED I LIKED IT BETTER AS A MARKER!
Hmmm...I KNOW I DON'T DARE WASTE TIME ON TRIVIALITIES...AND YET, HOW CAN I TELL WHAT IS TRIVIAL, AND WHAT'S NOT?
ALL THE EVIDENCE POINTS TO THE FACT THAT SOMETHING IN MY CITADEL MAY CAUSE THE EARTH'S DESTRUCTION IN LESS THAN AN HOUR--AND RIGHT NOW, IT COULD BE ANYTHING, AS FAR AS I KNOW!
INCLUDING, NOW THAT I THINK OF IT-- ME!
GOT TO MAKE CERTAIN THAT I MYSELF DON'T BRING ANYTHING INTO THE FORTRESS WHICH COULD SOMEHOW CAUSE A FATAL CHAIN REACTION!
WELL, THIS SUPER-BLOWTORCH OF MINE SHOULD TAKE CARE OF ANY FATAL SPACE-DUST OR THE LIKE!
BESIDES, NOTHING LIKE A NICE HOT SHOWER ANYWAY!
14

I'M NOT EVEN WASTING UNDUE TIME, SINCE I'M MOVING AT SUPER-SPEED!
EVEN WALKING THIS WAY, I'D BE NOTHING BUT A RED-AND-BLUE BLUR TO LOIS OR BATMAN, IF THEY WERE HERE NOW!
THUS, IT'S BEEN ONLY A FEW SECONDS SINCE I TOUCHED DOWN OUTSIDE--
YET HERE I AM, ALREADY AT MY DISINTEGRATION PIT!
"IT'S A SORT OF ATOMIC CAULDRON, REALLY... FUELED BY RADIOACTIVE KRYPTONIAN ELEMENTS I OBTAINED FROM THE BOTTLE-CITY OF KANDOR, LONG AGO.
"IT'LL DISSOLVE ALMOST ANYTHING WHICH IS DROPPED INTO IT BACK INTO ITS MOLECULAR COMPONENTS -- WITHIN AN INSTANT--
--AND THAT WOULD INCLUDE YOURS TRULY, IF I WERE FEELING SUICIDAL.
STILL, MY X-RAY VISION REVEALS NO HINT OF ANYTHING WRONG--EITHER HERE AT THE SURFACE OR AT PIT'S BOTTOM.
THERE ARE NO NATURAL FAULTS HEREABOUTS--AND I DON'T DETECT ANY MAN-MADE ONES, EITHER.
GOT TO THINK, THOUGH:
COULD THE DISINTEGRATION PIT, SOMEHOW, BE THE EARTH-DESTROYING MENACE I'M LOOKING FOR??
15

"I CAN'T SEE HOW--UNLESS IT GOT OUT OF CONTROL, SOMEHOW, AS HAPPENED ONLY ONCE--"*
CAREFUL, SUPERGIRL! WE PROMISED THE U.N. DISARMAMENT COMMISSION NOT TO LOSE A SINGLE ONE OF THESE OUTLAWED WEAPONS!
RIGHT YOU ARE, COUSIN KAL-EL!
ONE SLIP--AND THE WHOLE WORLD MIGHT BE POLLUTED--OR EVEN OBLITERATED!
*ACTION #402. --Len
"SOON, IN THESE ROCKY DEPTHS BENEATH THE FORTRESS..."
FIRST I'LL DESTROY THIS "JIGSAW-RAY" GUN, WHICH CAN DISMANTLE A CITY IN SECONDS.
I'LL TOSS IN THIS EARTHQUAKE-CAUSING SEISMOTRON--
--OH YES, AND THIS VAPOR BOMB USED BY A DICTATOR TO BRAINWASH HIS SUBJECTS!
"THEN, EVEN AS WE FINISHED--"
HOLD IT, KARA! MY X-RAY VISION SHOWS YOU HID SOME KIND OF DEADLY LASER PISTOL!
OH!
AND HOW ABOUT THAT CRYOGEN FREEZE-WAVE PROJECTOR YOU SECRETE OVER THERE, YOU SUPER-RAT!
"SUDDENLY, AT THAT MOMENT, MY KRYPTONIAN COUSIN AND I HATED EACH OTHER WITH EVERY FIBRE OF OUR BEINGS..."
YOU ASKED FOR IT, YOU FEMALE JUDAS!
THIS IS WHERE YOU GET YOURS, YOU BENEDICT ARNOLD!
"IT WAS A WILD IRRATIONA WAR WE FOUGH
"...IN WHICH EACH OF US ATTACKED ALSO THE THINGS THE OTHER ONE LOVED:"
THIS TWIN-HEADED BIRD SHE HAD BROUGHT FROM THE PLANET DUPLOR--
--WHERE LIFE FORMS MUTATED AND EVOLVED LIKE SIAMESE TWINS!
I WAS READY TO SMASH IT TO BIT IN ITS CRYSTAL CAGE--
--EVEN THOUG TO DO SO WOULD BE TO BREAK MY CO AGAINST KILLIN

"I HELD BACK FROM THAT ACT OF DESTRUCTION--BUT MOMENTS LATER, I MANAGED TO ENRAGE SUPERGIRL SO THAT SHE FLEW AT ME ABOVE THE ATOMIC CAULDRON, AND--"
I--I'M FALLING!! EYAHHHH!
HAH! YOU FORGOT TO STAY BEHIND THE PRO-TECTIVE RIM!
THE RADIOACTIVE KRYPTONIAN FUEL IN THAT FURNACE AFFECTS YOU ALMOST THE WAY ORDINARY RADIATION WOULD AFFECT A NORMAL EARTH-BEING!
"YET, EVEN AS KARA FACED CERTAIN DOOM, A DEEPER INSTINCT SURGED WITHIN ME..."
WH-WHAT AM I DOING??
I CAN'T STAND BY AND WATCH HER DIE!
MUCH AS I HATE HER--SHE IS MY OWN FLESH AND BLOOD!
"THEN, AFTER I'D RESCUED HER..."
I DON'T EXPECT ANY GRATITUDE! I DON'T KNOW WHY I DESPISE YOU SO, BUT--
WAIT! ALL OF A SUDDEN-- I THINK I DO KNOW WHY WE HATE EACH OTHER!
QUICK! WE'VE GOT TO GET OUT OF HERE!
"SHORTLY, IN THE OPEN AIR..."
WHY--I CAN FEEL THAT AWFUL HATRED LEAVING ME--BUT HOW--?
THIS BIRD, KARA! ORDINARILY, ITS TWO HEADS WORK AS A PERFECT TEAM!
I KNEW WHATEVER WAS AFFECTING US--
--MUST BE AFFECTING IT, AS WELL!
WE'D BEEN SO BUSY FIGHTING, WE HADN'T NOTICED THOSE FUMES PERMEATING THE FORTRESS.
THEY MUST BE FROM THE BRAINWASH BOMB WE TOSSED INTO THE DISINTEGRATION PIT BEFORE.
IT MUST HAVE CONTAINED A HATE GAS WHICH COMBINED WITH THE KRYPTONIAN ELEMENTS THERE--AND AFFECTED OUR MINDS!
BOY, DO I FEEL LIKE A FOOL!
DON'T WE BOTH!
BUT--WHAT ABOUT TODAY'S EVEN MORE DEVASTATING THREAT?
17

THE ENTIRE PLANET'S IN DANGER--MY FORTRESS OF SOLITUDE IS SOMEHOW RESPONSIBLE--YET I DON'T KNOW HOW!
I CAN'T EVEN DESTROY IT AS A PREVENTIVE MEASURE--BECAUSE I CAN'T BE SURE THAT WOULDN'T BE PRECISELY THE ACTION WHICH WOULD TRIGGER THE EXPLOSION!
YET, TO TAKE NO ACTION AT ALL--MAY BE EQUALLY FATAL!
GOT TO KEEP THINKING--PROBING--WORKING AGAINST THE CLOCK!
Ah, CAN YOU ENVISION IT, DEAR ROGER?
CAN YOU SEE SUPERMAN IN YOUR MIND'S EYE, AS I CAN?
CAN YOU IMAGINE THE INNER AGONY H MUST FEEL-FACING THE IMPOSSIBILITY OF CHANGING THE FUTURE?
I CAN'T--I DON'T DARE BELIEVE THAT THERE'S NO ANSWER TO THE DILEMMA POSED BY DOMINUS AND HIS STRANGE METEOR!
I REFUSE TO ADMIT THAT I'M DAMNED IF I DO--AND DAMNED IF I DON'T!
I HAVE TO BELIEVE I'M MASTER OF MY FATE--NOT ITS HELPLESS PAWN!
AND IF THERE IS AN ANSWER, THIS IS THE ONLY WAY I CAN HOPE TO FIND IT IN TIME--
--BY CONTINUING TO INVENTORY THE VARIOUS CHAMBERS OF MY FORTRESS--
--LOOKING FOR SOME CLUE--ANY CLUE--AS TO WHAT MIGHT CAUSE THE WHOLE PLACE TO EXPLODE IN LESS THAN AN HOUR!
18

AND THAT IS EXACTLY AS I WANTED IT TO BE!
NOT ONLY SHALL EARTH BE DESTROYED--BUT SUPERMAN WILL CONSIDER HIMSELF RESPONSIBLE FOR ITS ANNIHILATION!
UH--I NEVER ASKED BEFORE, DOMINUS--BUT WHAT ABOUT US WHEN THE EARTH'S GONE?
WOULDN'T IT BE BETTER TO CONQUER THE WORLD THAN TO DESTROY IT?
YOU THINK SMALL, ROGER... LIKE ALL LESSER MEN!
THERE ARE COUNTLESS EARTHS IN THE MULTIVERSE--PARALLEL WORLDS TO RAVAGE AND REND--ALMOST ALL OF THEM WITHOUT A "SUPERMAN"!
NOW YOU'RE TALKING!
BUT, BOY, I'LL BE GLAD WHEN THIS HOUR'S OVER--AND WE KNOW WE'VE WON!
OF COURSE WE'VE WON, FOOL! IT'S ONLY A MATTER OF TIME--
--ABOUT FIFTY MINUTES, TO BE MORE PRECISE!
PERHAPS IT'S SOMETHING HERE IN MY SUPER-WEAPONS ROOM, WHERE I STORE DEATH-DEVICES I'VE CONFISCATED FROM VILLAINS OF MANY A WORLD!
BUT I'VE CHECKED AND RE-CHECKED EACH OF THEM, MANY TIMES OVER, TO BE CERTAIN THEY'RE NON-OPERATIONAL!
BESIDES, THAT WOULD BE SO OBVIOUS--
--AND, TO THE EXTENT THAT I CAN GAUGE DOMINUS AT ALL, HE'S A MOST DEVIOUS OPPONENT!
19

EVEN MY ARCH-FOE LEX LUTHOR NEVER POSED ME ANY MORE MAD-DENING PROBLEM...
...AND I'VE FOUGHT HIM OFTEN ENOUGH TO GIVE HIM HIS OWN CHAMBER HERE!
EARTHQUAKE MAKER
MONEY MAGNET
ATOMIC DEATH RAY
LUTHOR
HMMM...I JUST WONDERED--COULD HE BE MASQUERADING AS THE MYSTERIOUS "DOMINUS"?
BUT NO! IF HE WERE TRYING TO DESTROY THE EARTH--HE'D WANT EVERYONE TO KNOW IT WAS HE!
THE ANSWER MUST LIE ELSEWHERE...!
GOOD THING I'VE GOT AN "INTERNAL CLOCK" WHICH IS AS PRECISE AS AN ATOMIC TIME-PIECE... SO THAT I CAN KEEP SEARCHING FOR A SOLUTION, RIGHT UP TO THE LAST SECOND.
BUT, WHAT HAPPENS IF THAT FINAL MOMENT ARRIVES--AND I STILL HAVEN'T--?
NO! I WON'T CONSIDER THE POSSIBILITY OF FAILURE! I CAN'T!!
MAYBE THE ANSWER LIES HERE IN MY KRYPTONIAN MEMORIAL--PAST THESE STATUES OF MY PARENTS, JOR-EL AND LARA.
I CARVED THESE STATUES MYSELF--FROM MY OWN SUPER-MEMORY.
I CAPTURE THEIR IMAGE ALMOST PE FECTLY--DO PRACTICALL TO THEIR FINGER-PRINTS!
SO WHY CAN'T I REMEMBER HOW I' BEEN CARELESS ENOUGH AT SOME TIME IN THE PAST TO LET A MAD SUPER VILLAIN PLANT WHA MAY BE A POWERFL TIME-BOMB IN MY OWN SANCTUM SANCTORUM?
JOR-EL
LARA

USED MY OWN
EMORY, TOO,
ERECT THIS
UGE HOLO-
CREEN...
...WHEREIN A THREE-DIMENSIONAL IMAGE OF MY NATIVE WORLD IS ACTIVATED BY THE BODY HEAT OF ANY-ONE WHO STANDS NEAR IT!

OVER AND OVER AGAIN, IT REPRODUCES THE LAST MOMENTS OF KRYPTON'S EXISTENCE...

...THE INSTANT WHEN A ROCKET DESIGNED BY MY FATHER CARRIED ME EARTH-WARD...

...ONLY SECONDS BEFORE KRYPTON ITSELF WAS TORN APART BY UNBELIEVABLE INTERNAL PRESSURES!
I RE-CREATED THE SCENE BY OVER-TAKING THE VERY LIGHT RAYS WHICH HAD EMANATED FROM KRYPTON...
...AND I'VE ALMOST GOT TO THE POINT WHERE IT NO LONGER TORTURES ME TO LOOK AT IT!

ND NOW, THE RE-
NACTMENT BEGINS
GAIN... AS IT WILL
SO LONG AS BOTH
ARTH AND THIS
ORTRESS STAND!
HAD NO REAL
ES WITH
RYPTON OTHER
AN MY PARENTS,
NCE I WAS AN
FANT WHEN
PERISHED!

BUT I HAVE FRIENDS HERE ON EARTH,... A GREAT MANY FRIENDS... DEAR FRIENDS...
...AT THE DAILY PLANET... AT GALAXY BROAD-CASTING... IN THE JUSTICE LEAGUE!

AND I DON'T KNOW IF I COULD BEAR THEIR LOSS, ON TOP OF THE DEATHS OF THE FACE-LESS BILLIONS.

I JUST... DON'T KNOW..!
21

BUT, THAT WAY LIES MADNESS... NOT ACTION!
IT'S THE LIVES OF PEOPLE LIKE LOIS LANE I'VE GOT TO THINK ABOUT... NOT THEIR DEATHS!
LOIS! IT SEEMS LIKE YESTER-DAY* THAT SHE FIRST CAME HERE, TO DO A PICTURE STORY ON THE FORTRESS...!
*ACTUALLY, IT WAS IN LOIS LANE #14. --Len
"I LEFT HER ALONE HERE IN THE KRYPTON EXHIBIT... WHICH RECREATES A TYPICAL KRYPTONIAN HOME, WITH EVERYTHING IN PERFECT WORKING ORDER...
SUPERMAN'S NOT BACK FROM METROPOLIS YET, AND IT'S BEDTIME!
GOOD! BY SPENDING A NIGHT HERE, I'LL PROVE TO HIM THIS WOULD BE A SAFE HOME FOR THE TWO OF US!
THEN HE WON'T HAVE ANY EXCUSE NOT TO MARR ME!
THIS BED CERTAINLY IS-- OHH! WHAT KIND OF A COUCH IS THIS?
NOW I REMEMBER! SUPERMAN SAID IT WAS A FLOATING ANTI-GRAVITY BED--
--BUT IT SEEMS MORE LIKE A FLYING CARPET TO ME!
UH OH! NOW A GUST OF AIR IS BLOWING IT OUT OF THE KRYPTON EXHIBIT!
I'LL CRASH SOMEWHERE-- I JUST KNOW IT!
SUPERMAN-- WHERE ARE YOU WHEN I NEED YOU!?
OOOF! TALK ABOUT YOUR HOMEGROWN IRONIES!
THE COUCH BUMPED INTO THAT SUPERMAN-ROBOT HE LEFT ON GUARD!
I'M OKAY FOR NOW--BUT MAYBE THIS FORTRESS ISN'T QUITE AS SAFE FOR ME AS I THOUGHT IT WAS!
POOR LOIS! SHE DIDN'T REALIZE THAT "GUST OF WIND" WAS MY DOING--TO DIS-COURAGE HER CHASING ME!
I DO CARE FOR HER, THOUGH-- FAR MORE THAN SHE KNOWS.
PERHAPS I COU TAKE HER AND A HANDFUL OF OTHERS TO ANOTHER EARTH-LIKE PLANET--WHER THEY'D SURVIVE, IF I FAILED TO--
NO! THAT KIND OF SOLUTION WORKED F MY FATHER JOR-EL...

...BUT IT'S NO GOOD FOR ME!
EARTH IS MY ADOPTED PLANET...AND I'M AS MUCH A PART OF IT AS IF I'D BEEN BORN HERE.
MY PARENTS WOULD UNDERSTAND, I'M SURE, IF THEY WERE STILL ALIVE!
FTER ALL, THEY LECTED TO ERISH WITH HEIR OWN WORLD, ATHER THAN RY TO FLEE IT.
Hmmm... NOT VERY LIKELY THAT WHATEVER BOOBY-TRAP DOMINUS HAS PLANTED IS HERE IN MY COMMUNICATIONS AREA, BUT I'D STILL BETTER CHECK IT OUT.
I'VE ALWAYS BEEN PROUD OF HOW ITS MONITOR SCREENS ALERT ME TO EMERGENCIES THE WORLD OVER!
THERE ARE EVEN HYPERSPACE RADIOS WHICH KEEP ME IN TOUCH WITH DISTANT WORLDS!
NOTHING TERRIBLY EXCITING GOING ON RIGHT NOW, THANK THE STARS... SINCE I SMASHED THAT METEOR.
ELSE, SOMEBODY WOULD COME ON TO--
--INTERRUPT THIS PROGRAM TO BRING YOU A SPECIAL NEWSBREAK BULLETIN!
UH-OH! NOW WHAT?
OH NO! IT CAN'T BE--!
HERE, LIVE BY HELICOPTER, IS THE FIRST FILM-FOOTAGE OF THE LONG-DORMANT VOLCANO KNOWN AS MT. HEPHAESTUS, WHICH HAS SUDDENLY ERUPTED--JUST AS MT. ST. HELEN'S DID IN THE STATE OF WASHINGTON, SOME MONTHS AGO...!
WHAT A TIME FOR THIS TO HAPPEN!
I MAY BE NEEDED TO HELP OUT--TO SAVE HUNDREDS, EVEN THOUSANDS OF HUMAN LIVES!
YET IF I DO--IT WOULD MEAN DELAYING MY SEARCH FOR THE TIME-BOMB THAT MIGHT COST FOUR BILLION LIVES!
23

FORTUNATELY, ALL INDICATIONS AT PRESENT ARE THAT THIS ERUPTION WILL BE FAR LESS VIOLENT THAN THE EARLIER ONE IN THE NORTHWEST.
AS OF THIS MOMENT, THERE ARE NO REPORTED DEATHS OR EVEN SERIOUS CASUALTIES... AND EVEN THE VOLCANO ITSELF SEEMS TO BE QUIETING DOWN...!
GOOD! THEN I WON'T BE NEEDED FOR THE NEXT HOUR, AND I CAN CONTINUE MY SUPER-SEARCH!
PRESUMPTUOUS OF ME, ANYWAY, TO THINK THAT PEOPLE CAN'T HANDLE MOST DISASTERS WITHOUT A SUPERMAN TO HOLD THEIR HANDS!
THEN, AS THE MAN OF STEEL EXITS FROM THE COMMUNCATIONS AREA, HE SUDDENLY NOTICES...
THOSE GAS-JETS! I'D FORGOTTEN ALL ABOUT THEM!
I'D BETTER MAKE SURE THEY'RE STILL FUNCTIONING PROPERLY!
I DESIGNED THEM TO RELEASE ANTI-BACTERIAL GAS ONCE A MONTH--
--TO DESTROY ANY DEADLY ALIEN MICROBES I MIGHT BRING BACK WITH ME FROM AN ADVENTURE IN OUTER SPACE.
YEP, THEY'RE IN WORKING ORDER, ALL RIGHT...
...AND THE GAS THEY'RE DUE TO RELEASE IN A HALF HOUR WILL SURELY KILL ANY MICROBES I MIGHT HAVE CARRIED BACK TO EARTH FROM THAT METEOR!
BESIDES, IT WAS AN EXPLOSION I SAW DOOMING THE EARTH--NOT SOME KIND OF GERM WARFARE!
24

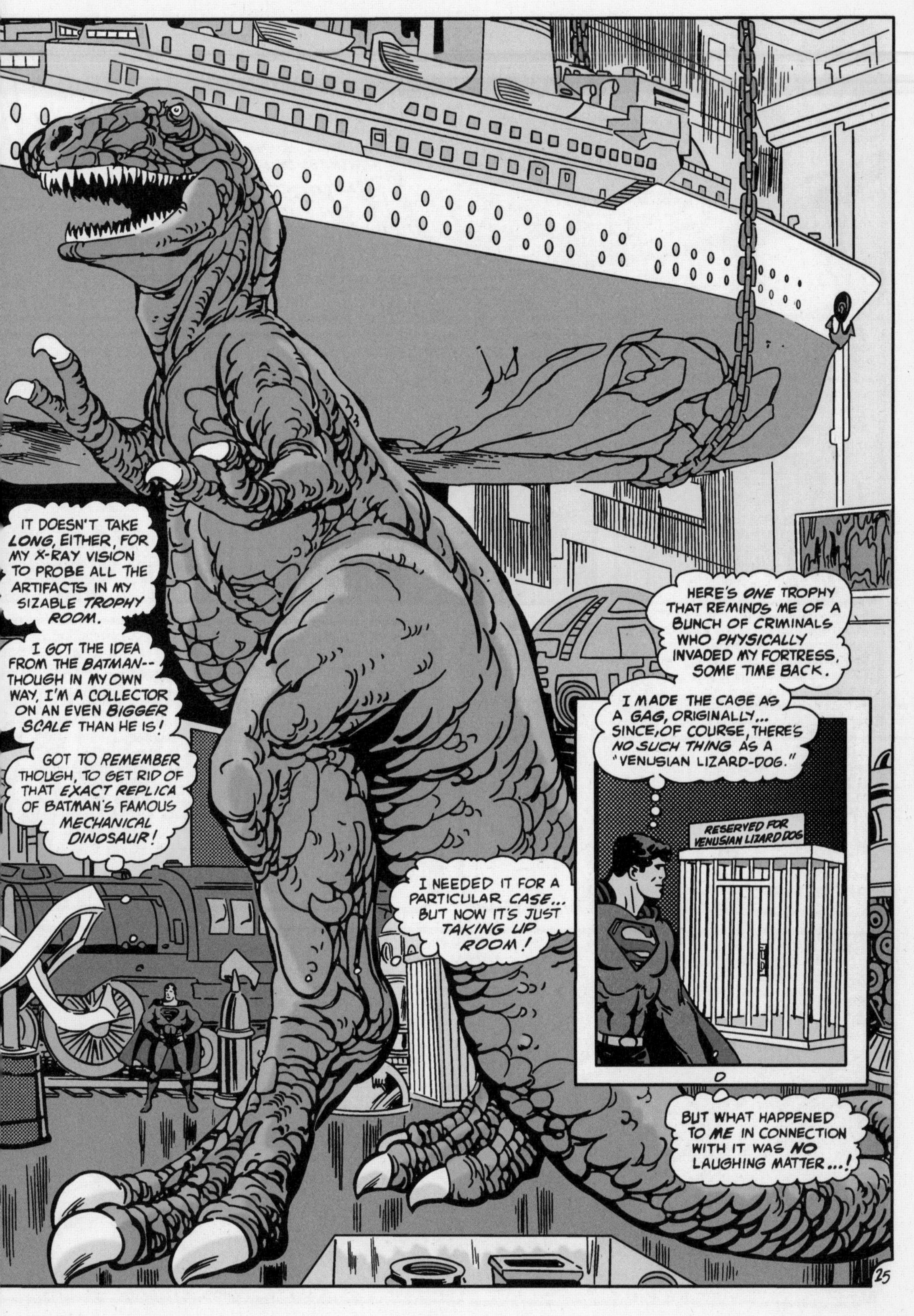

IT DOESN'T TAKE LONG, EITHER, FOR MY X-RAY VISION TO PROBE ALL THE ARTIFACTS IN MY SIZABLE TROPHY ROOM.
I GOT THE IDEA FROM THE BATMAN-- THOUGH IN MY OWN WAY, I'M A COLLECTOR ON AN EVEN BIGGER SCALE THAN HE IS!
GOT TO REMEMBER THOUGH, TO GET RID OF THAT EXACT REPLICA OF BATMAN'S FAMOUS MECHANICAL DINOSAUR!
I NEEDED IT FOR A PARTICULAR CASE... BUT NOW IT'S JUST TAKING UP ROOM!
HERE'S ONE TROPHY THAT REMINDS ME OF A BUNCH OF CRIMINALS WHO PHYSICALLY INVADED MY FORTRESS, SOME TIME BACK.
I MADE THE CAGE AS A GAG, ORIGINALLY... SINCE, OF COURSE, THERE'S NO SUCH THING AS A "VENUSIAN LIZARD-DOG."
RESERVED FOR VENUSIAN LIZARD DOG
BUT WHAT HAPPENED TO ME IN CONNECTION WITH IT WAS NO LAUGHING MATTER...!
25

"A HOODLUM NAMED 'KING' ANDREWS HAD LEARNED MY CITADEL'S LOCATION WHEN HE'D CRASHED NEARBY--AND SEEN ME RUSHING OUT TO RESCUE HIM.*
"LATER, WITH HIS SON MICHAEL AND A MYSTERIOUS ELECTRONICS EXPERT NAMED SLESAR, HE CAPTURED CLARK KENT AS A POSSIBLE HOSTAGE, AND..."
GENTLEMEN--SUPERMAN'S FORTRESS OF SOLITUDE!
YOU DID IT, DAD!
"I COULDN'T ACT W
OUT EXPOSING MY
SECRET IDENTITY, B
I FIGURED THEY'D
NEVER MAKE IT PAS
THE DOOR.
* SEE ACTION #407. --Len
"I'D RECKONED WITHOUT THE ONE CALLED SLESAR..."
THERE! I'VE DEACTIVATED HIS PROTECTIVE DEVICES, ELECTRONICALLY!
"SOON, INSIDE..."
GOOD WORK, SLESAR! MIKE--YOU GUARD KENT! HE'S OUR ONLY TICKET OUT OF HERE IF SUPERMAN SHOWS UP!
KEEP HIM IN THAT EMPTY CAGE
WHILE ME AND SLESAR LOOK FO
GOODIES TO LOO
RESERVED FOR VENUSIAN LIZARD-DOG
"MINUTES LATER..."
MY DISASTER MONITOR'S PICKING UP AN SOS FROM THE SAHARA!
GOT TO GET OUT OF HERE!
MIKE! LEAVE KENT AND COME HERE! I NEED YOU!
COMING, DAD!
MY SUPER-VENTRILOQUISM
STUNT WILL GIVE ME ABOU
TEN SECONDS
...WHICH I JUST PRAY IS ENOUGH TO SAVE BOTH THOSE SAHARAN OIL-RIGGERS BELOW--AND MY SECRET IDENTITY!
MOST OF THAT OIL DERRICK'S BEEN EATEN AWAY BY SOME SORT OF SUPER-POTENT ACID--THE RESULT OF POLLUTION WHICH WORKED ITSELF UNDERGROUND!
I CAN'T LET IT SPREAD!

Y SUPER-SPEED WHIPS UP TORNADO OF SAND, URROUNDING THE GUSHING FLOW OF ACID.
NEXT, I'LL USE MY HEAT VISION TO FUSE THE SAND PARTICLES TOGETHER TO FORM A SUPER-HARD COCOON OF SILICON...
...AND I'LL CIRCULATE THE DEADLY ACID RIGHT BACK INTO THE UNDERGROUND POOL IT CAME FROM!
THIS DONE, I GOT BACK JUST IN TIME..."
STILL THERE, HUH, KENT?
RESERVED FOR VENUSIAN LIZARD-DOG
ROM NOW N, I'M NOT UDGING!
"I'D HOPED FOR NO MORE CRISES, BUT--"
NOT AGAIN! AN EMERGENCY IN FLORIDA THIS TIME!
THIS CALLS FOR A MORE DRASTIC PLOY!
MIKE HEARS NOTHING-- BUT THIS IS AN ULTRA-SONIC WHISTLE...
...SO INTENSE, IT SETS UP SHARP VIBRATIONS IN THE CEILING ABOVE, THAT SHOULD CAUSE A--
-MASSIVE CAVE-IN!
TH-THE WHOLE CEILING'S COMING DOWN!
"THEN, AFTER TONS OF ROCK AND DEBRIS HAD SETTLED..."
MR. KENT! ARE YOU ALL RIGHT?
SAY SOMETHING!!
"HE THOUGHT I HAD DIED IN THE CAVE-IN... OR ELSE WOULD SWIFTLY SUFFOCATE...
"BUT OF COURSE, I WAS NO LONGER INSIDE THE RUBBLE...
"...BUT RATHER, THOUSANDS OF MILES AWAY, ALREADY PLUNGING INTO THE DEPTHS OF THE ATLANTIC...!"
A DISABLED POLARIS SUB SENT THAT SOS BECAUSE IT WAS SNAGGED BY SOME KIND OF MONSTROUS SEAWEED.
WELL, AQUAMAN HIMSELF COULDN'T MAKE BETTER USE OF THIS PAIR OF SWORDFISH TO CUT THEM LOOSE!
27

"MEANWHILE, THE THREE INTRUDERS WERE SHOWING THEIR TRUE COLORS..."
BUT, DAD-- WE CAN'T LEAVE MR. KENT IN THERE--HE'LL RUN OUT OF AIR!
LET HIM! WE DON'T NEED HIM ANY MORE!
I WAS GOING TO KILL HIM, ANYWAY!
JUST AS I'M GOING TO KILL BOTH OF YOU!

SLESAR! WHAT THE DEVIL DO YOU THINK YOU ARE DOING!?
NOT "SLESAR," YOU FOOL--

--BUT LEX LUTHOR!
SUPERMAN'S NUMBER ONE ARCH-ENEMY!
I KNEW YOU'D NEVER HAVE TAKEN ME INTO THE FORTRESS--SO I HAD TO BECOME "SLESAR."

BUT I WASN'T IN IT FOR THE MONEY!
NO, WHILE YOU WERE BUSY COLLECTING SPACE-JEWEL AND TRINKETS, I METIC-ULOUSLY PLANTED A DEADLY BOMB WHERE SUPERMAN HIMSELF IS SURE TO SET IT OFF!
MORE THAN ANYTHIN ELSE IN THE WORLD, I WANTED HIM AND HI FORTRESS ANNIHILATED
I PLAN TO BE LONG GONE BEFORE THE BIG BANG--BUT FIRST I MUST SILENCE BOTH OF YOU!

NOBODY DOUBLE-CROSSES KING ANDREWS--NOT EVEN LUTHOR! I--
DAD!
AARRRRH!
"KING ANDREWS WAS DEAD--AND HIS SON MICHAEL WAS NEXT ON LUTHOR'S LIST--

"--WHEN I ARRIVED JUST IN TIME TO TEAR UP THAT LIST!"
SUPERMAN!
WHO ELSE?
AND RIGHT ON TIME, TOO!
UHHHH

"THEN, AS NOW, I BEGAN A
RANTIC, SUPER-FAST SEARCH
OR A DEADLY TIME-BOMB.
"ONLY THING IS, THAT TIME I KNEW I WAS DEFINITELY LOOKING FOR SUCH A BOMB..."
HE SOUND OF A DETONATOR ICKING--INSIDE MY KEYHOLE!
TICKING--AND BEING ACTIVATED BY MY VERY PRESENCE!
"... AND SO I FOUND IT.

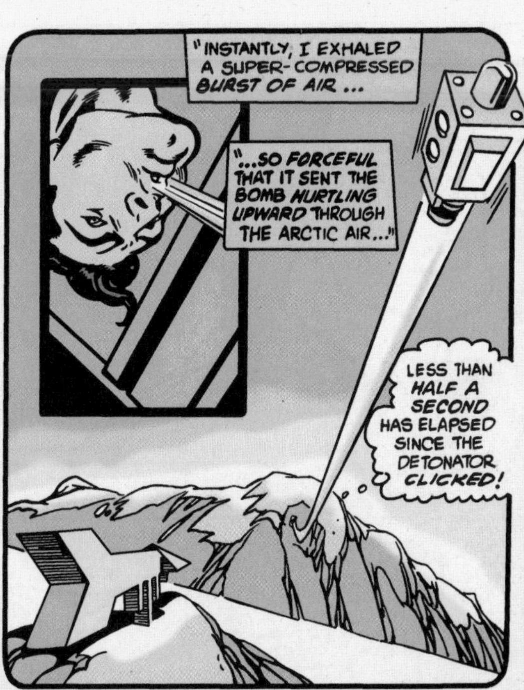
"INSTANTLY, I EXHALED A SUPER-COMPRESSED BURST OF AIR ...
"...SO FORCEFUL THAT IT SENT THE BOMB HURTLING UPWARD THROUGH THE ARCTIC AIR..."
LESS THAN HALF A SECOND HAS ELAPSED SINCE THE DETONATOR CLICKED!

"...TO EXPLODE IN OUTER SPACE!"
WOW! THAT BLAST WAS CREATED BY ANTI-MATTER FUSION... WHICH WOULD'VE OBLITERATED EVEN ME!

OU WOULD HAVE LET THE OMB EXPLODE HERE-- ND SACRIFICED EVEN OUR OWN LIFE--JUST S LONG AS I DIED, TOO!
LUTHOR, DO YOU REALLY HATE ME THAT MUCH?
YOU ALREADY KNOW THE ANSWER TO THAT, SUPERMAN!
"INDEED I DID... TO MY ETERNAL SORROW.

SOON, AFTER GIVING KING ANDREWS A PROPER BURIAL..."
UPERMAN! I JUST REALIZED-- VE FORGOT MR. KENT!
DON'T ORRY, MIKE!
RESERVED FOR VENUSIAN LIZARD-DOG
er... AFTER THE CAVE-IN, I HAD ENOUGH TIME TO TUNNEL HIM OUT OF THE CAGE, AND AWAY TO SAFETY!

THAT WAS BY FAR THE CLOSEST CALL EITHER I OR THE FORTRESS OF SOLITUDE HAS EVER HAD.
NOW, HOWEVER, ALL THAT REMAINS OF THAT "INVASION" IS A GRAVESTONE OUTSIDE...
...AND NO MAN KNOWS JUST WHERE IT LIES!
KING ANDREWS
RESERVED FOR VENUSIAN LIZARD-DOG
29

AND, LUTHOR'S IN PRISON-- I MADE SURE OF THAT WITH MY X-RAY VISION ON THE WAY BACK HERE--
--WHILE THE MENACE POSED TO THE EARTH WAS OBVIOUSLY PLANNED AND EXECUTED BY SOMEONE VERY MUCH AT LARGE!
WELL, JUST ONE PLACE LEFT ON THIS FIRST LEVEL TO CHECK OUT...
...NAMELY, THE SPECIAL MODULAR APARTMENT I BUILT ONTO THE FORTRESS FOR MY COUSIN, KARA...
...A.K.A. SUPERGIR
I DON'T LIKE INVADING HE PRIVACY WHILE SHE'S NOT HERE- BUT THIS IS EMERGENCY
"BESIDES, SHE GAVE ME PERMISSION TO ENTER HER ROOMS- AFTER OUR FUME-INDUCED LITTLE SUPER-FEUD ENDED
I SURE DON'T NEED THIS DOOR ANY MORE!
IT'S ONE FORTRESS FOR BOTH OF US-- SHARE AND SHARE ALIKE!
"SUPERGIRL"! IT'S A NAME THAT'S BEEN GOOD ENOUGH, THESE PAST SEVERAL YEARS SINCE SHE ARRIVED FROM A LAST SURVIVING FRAGMENT OF KRYPTON--
BUT ONE OF THESE FINE DAYS, IT'S GOING TO HAVE TO BE CHANGED-- TO SUPERWOMAN!
HOW COULD I EVER FORGET THE LONG MONTHS I SPENT TRAINING HER FOR LIFE ON EARTH--
"--OR THE ALMOST-PATERNAL PRIDE I FELT THAT DAY WHEN IT WAS I, NOT DOMINUS, WHO INTERRUPTED ALL TELECASTS ON THE PLANET TO ANNOUNCE:"
FOR SOME TIME NOW, I'VE BEEN AIDED SECRETLY BY MY "EMERGENCY SECRET WEAPON"...
AND HERE SHE IS... MY LOVELY, SUPER-POWERFUL COUSIN, SUPERGIRL!
HELLO, EVERYBODY!

UT--CAN'T LET MYSELF
VAX NOSTALGIC
BOUT COUSIN KARA.
TIME'S RUNNING OUT, AND I'VE ONLY EXAMINED THE FIRST LEVEL OF THE FORTRESS!
MAYBE THE ANSWER I'M LOOKING FOR-- THE ANSWER I MUST FIND--IS UP HERE ON THE SECOND!
I'LL START WITH MY LAB, EVEN THOUGH EVERYTHING HERE HAS BEEN CHECKED OUT MANY TIMES, TO BE CERTAIN IT POSES NO DANGER.
FUNNY HOW, EVERY TIME I COME HERE, I STILL EXPECT TO SEE THE BOTTLE-CITY OF KANDOR...
...RESTING ON THIS PEDESTAL WHERE IT SAT FOR YEARS...
"I GUESS I SHOULD BE GRATEFUL THAT THE MAD, HUMANOID SUPER-COMPUTER CALLED BRAINIAC WAS THEN JOURNEYING THROUGH SPACE, 'COLLECTING' CITIES OF VARIOUS PLANETS BY FIRST SHRINKING THEM DOWN.
"ONE OF THE CITIES HE CHOSE TO 'COLLECT' WAS METROPOLIS--AND I MADE SURE CLARK KENT WAS THERE AT THE TIME.
"I'M EVEN LUCKIER THAT HE DECIDED TO MINIATURIZE AND STEAL A DOZEN GREAT EARTH-CITIES, AS WELL, TO ADD TO HIS BIZARRE COLLECTION.
"AFTER THE MADMAN HAD SHRUNK METROPOLIS AND PLACED IT IN A BOTTLE, I WAS ABLE TO FLY OUT..."
NOW TO REPLACE THE CORK, SO BRAINIAC DOESN'T NOTICE--AND SUSPECT I'M NOW INSIDE HIS SHIP!
31

THIS IS HIS HYPER-FORCE MACHINE!
GOT TO STUDY IT CAREFULLY-- FIGURE OUT A WAY TO MAKE IT RETURN THOSE CITIES TO EARTH!

"UNFORTUNATELY, BRAINIAC HAD AN ALIEN PET ALONG FOR COMPANY, AND
I HAVEN'T LOOKED AT MY PRIZE CITY FOR AWHILE.
THAT BUZZING FLY ANNOYS ME! SWAT HIM, KOKO!

GOOD THING BRAINIAC DIDN'T LOOK CLOSELY AT THIS "FLY"!
I'LL HIDE IN THIS BOTTLE HE JUST UNCORKED--TILL HIS PET PUTS AWAY THAT SWATTER!

G-GREAT STARS! THAT'S A CITY OF KRYPTON--MY HOME PLANET!
BRAINIAC MUST HAVE IMPRISONED IT INSIDE HIS BOTTLE YEARS BE-FORE KRYPTON EX-PLODED, SO THAT--

OOOF! I CAN'T FLY IN HERE! OF COURSE!
KRYPTON'S GRAVITY CONDITIONS ARE DUPLICATED HERE-- SO I HAVE NO SUPER-POWERS AS I DO ON EARTH!

"REGAINING MY COMPOSURE, I SOUGHT OUT A KRYPTONIAN SCIENTIST FOR THE FIRST TIME IN MY LIFE..."
--AND MY FATHER WAS JOR-EL, THE FAMOUS SCIENTIST!
I KNEW HIM WELL! I'M PROFESSOR KIMDA-- AND THIS IS KANDOR, THE CITY WHICH WAS ONCE KRYPTON'S CAPITAL.

"PROFESSOR KIMDA, IT SEEMS, HAD USED HIS TELESCOPE TO STUDY BRAINIAC'S CONTROL DEVICE..."
NORMALIZING HYPER-FORCE
BOTTLE #1
BOTTLE #2
BOTTLE #3
BOTTLE #4
I'M MADE A CHART OF THE BUTTONS THAT CAN RESTORE THE MINIATURE CITIES TO EARTH!

"SOON AFTERWARD, BRAINIAC DECIDED TO GO HOME--SO HE PUT HIMSELF AND HIS PET INTO SUSPENDED ANIMATION...
"...HIS MOST PRECIOUS BOTTLE-CITY BY HIS SIDE.

"THIS WAS OUR CHANCE! I COULDN'T FLY AS LONG AS I STAYED IN THE BOTTLE-CITY...
..BUT KIMDA ROVIDED ME TH A POWERFUL ROCKET HICH GOT ME UP TO ITS METAL CORK.

"AND I'D BROUGHT ALONG A METAL-EATING MOLE FROM KANDOR'S ZOO..."
HE'LL BURROW A TUNNEL BIG ENOUGH FOR ME TO CLIMB THROUGH.

NOW THAT I'M OUT-SIDE, I'M FREE OF THE KRYPTONIAN GRAVITY WITHIN!
I CAN FLY TO BRAINIAC'S CONTROL PANEL--

--AND EACH BUTTON I PRESS WILL MAKE A CITY REAPPEAR BACK ON EARTH, UNHARMED, AT NORMAL SIZE!

HEN, SUDDENLY--A DILEMMA--!"
ANSMITTING THE ARTH-CITIES BACK AS DRAINED THE ATTERIES OF HEIR COSMIC POWER.
NLY ONE CHARGE F HYPER-FORCE LEFT--
ENOUGH TO RESTORE KANDOR TO NORMAL SIZE OR ME--BUT NOT BOTH!

WELL, I'M ONLY ONE MAN! THE HYPER-RAY CAN SAVE A MILLION PEOPLE IN THE KRYPTONIAN CITY--ALLOWING THEM TO LIVE ON EARTH.
I'LL PRESS THE BUTTON THAT WILL LIBERATE THEM...!

"BEFORE I COULD REACH THE BUTTON, HOWEVER..."
WHAT? THAT TINY ROCKET "PUNCHED" THE BUTTON AHEAD OF ME--AND THE RAY STRUCK ME!
I'M REGAINING NORMAL SIZE SWIFTLY!

T'S I--KIMDA! I FLEW THE ROCKET OUT OF THE HOLE IN THE CORK TO PUNCH THE BUTTON, KNOWING THAT ONLY ONE CHARGE WOULD BE LEFT!
WE OF KANDOR COULD NOT LET THE EARTH--NAY, THE UNIVERSE--BE DEPRIVED OF ITS GREATEST HERO!
YOU SACRIFICED YOUR PEOPLE--FOR ME!
I'M GRATEFUL--BUT NOW YOUR CITY MUST REMAIN FOREVER TINY!
33

LET BRAINIAC'S SHIP FLY ON!
WHEN HE AWAKENS, HE'LL HAVE NO STOLEN CITIES!

"AND SOON, BACK HERE IN MY FORTRESS...!
THE MINIATURE KRYPTONIAN CITY WILL KEEP SAFELY HERE.

PERHAPS I'LL FIND A WAY TO RESTORE IT TO NORMAL SIZE ONE DAY-- AND LIVE WITH MY OWN PEOPLE AGAIN.
SOMEDAY! WHO KNOWS...

AND, AMAZINGLY, THAT "SOMEDAY" DID COME TO PASS! *
MONTHS AGO, I FOUND A WAY TO ENLARGE THE KANDORIANS AND THEIR CITY AGAIN-- ON A LARGE PRIMITIVE PLANET ORBITING A RED SUN SUCH AS KRYPTON ITSELF ONCE CIRCLED.
UNKNOWN TO ME, THEY HAD DELIBERATELY CHOSEN A PHASE-WORLD, ONE WHICH TRULY EXISTS ONLY IN ANOTHER DIMENSION...
...AND WHICH ONLY APPEARS IN THIS DIMENSION DURING A SHIFT IN THE COSMIC AXIS.
BUT WHENEVER IT DOES POP UP, I'LL BE RIGHT THERE WAITING TO PAY NEW KANDOR A VISIT--
--PROVIDING I'M STILL ALIVE!
* SEE SUPERMAN #338. --Len.

NO! I DON'T DARE CONSIDER THAT POSSIBILITY--BECAUSE IF I'M DEAD LESS THAN A HALF-HOUR FROM NOW, THAT MEANS THE EARTH WILL BE, TOO!
NEXT STOP--MY KRYPTONITE STORAGE ROOM!

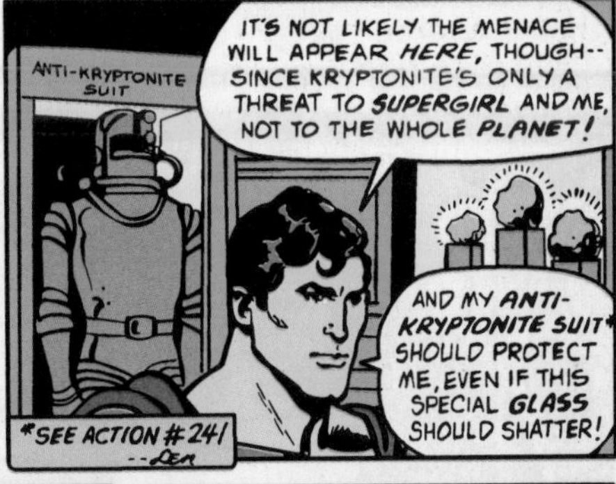
ANTI-KRYPTONITE SUIT
IT'S NOT LIKELY THE MENACE WILL APPEAR HERE, THOUGH--SINCE KRYPTONITE'S ONLY A THREAT TO SUPERGIRL AND ME, NOT TO THE WHOLE PLANET!
AND MY ANTI-KRYPTONITE SUIT* SHOULD PROTECT ME, EVEN IF THIS SPECIAL GLASS SHOULD SHATTER!
*SEE ACTION #241 --Len

NOTHING SEEMS OUT OF ORDER IN MY ROBOT STORAGE ROOM, EITHER!
I TRY TO KEEP UP TO DATE ON THE LATEST IN ROBOTICS--
--EVEN THOUGH KARA AND I RARELY USE OUR ROBOT DOUBLES THESE DAYS!

IT ONLY TAKES ME A FEW SECONDS TO CHECK MY SUPER-COMPUTER ROOM, AS WELL--AND EVERYTHING SEEMS SHIPSHAPE!
HANDY LITTLE THING! IN ADDITION TO STORING MORE INFORMATION THAN ANY OTHER COMPUTER ON EARTH--
--IT'S CONNECTED TO ARCHIVES WHICH INCLUDE PERHAPS THE LARGEST CRIME FILE ON EARTH.

I USE THE OTHER HALF OF MY ROOM FOR MY PHANTOM ZONE VIEWER.
MAYBE I'D BETTER CHECK IN ON THAT DIMENSION'S UNWILLING GUESTS...
...JUST TO BE CERTAIN ONE OF THEM HASN'T ESCAPED SOMEHOW, AND BECOME DOMINUS.

OPE, LOOKS LIKE THEY'RE LL ACCOUNTED FOR--SOME OF THE MOST ANGEROUS CRIMINALS FROM DEAD KRYPTON OR ANYPLACE ELSE IN THE KNOWN UNIVERSE!
HERE'S MON-EL, TOO--REALLY LAR GAND OF THE PLANET DAXAM--WHOM I ONCE THOUGHT WAS MY LONG-LOST BROTHER!
HE DOESN'T BELONG IN THERE WITH THOSE OTHER DO-BADDERS... AND I'LL NEVER GIVE UP TRYING TO FIND A WAY TO FREE HIM FROM THE PHANTOM ZONE...
...BUT I CAN'T WORRY ABOUT THAT NOW!*
*MON-EL WAS FINALLY FREED--IN THE 30TH CENTURY--BY THE FAMED LEGION OF SUPER-HEROES. --Len
35

TIME'S RUNNING OUT-- AND I STILL SEEM AS MUCH IN THE DARK AS EVER!
I'M ALMOST TEMPTED TO SKIP TAKING A MAGICAL MYSTERY TOUR OF MY ALIEN ZOO!
BUT I DONT DARE RISK OVERLOOKING A CLUE-- NO MATTER HOW SMALL!
THESE TWO EXHIBITS HAVE ALWAYS BEEN MY FAVORITES: A GIANT INSECT AND THOSE MINI-DINOSAURS!...
...FROM A WORLD WHERE EVOLUTION WORKED A WEE BIT DIFFERENTLY THAN ON EARTH.

I'VE ALWAYS HAD A SOFT SPOT FOR THIS DANCING PLANT, TOO!
I FOUND IT ON MARS--BUT IT REALLY CAME FROM A SPORE THAT HAD DRIFTED THERE FROM ANOTHER GALAXY!
IT'S GOOD COMPAN THOUGH..
...FOR THIS "VENUS BUTTERFLY," AS I CALL IT, WHICH SINGS LIKE A CANARY!
IT MAY BE THE APHRODITE OF INSECTS-- BUT ITS REAL HOME WAS ON A PLANET OF THE STAR BETELGEUSE!

THIS ONE, I'LL ADMIT, I'D JUST AS SOON DONATE ELSEWHERE:
I CALL IT THE BRAVADO-BEAST, BECAUSE IT HATES THE COLOR YELLOW!
THE MERE SIGHT OF MY BELT OR EMBLEM ALWAYS SENDS IT INTO A RAGE.

"LOIS ONCE THOUGHT ME A COWARD BECAUSE I HID BEHIND HER WHEN IT CHARGED ME*...
"BUT IT CALMED DOWN, WHEN IT DIDN'T SEE YELLOW."
*LOIS LANE #14. --ESH

IT'S REALLY EVEN LESS DANGEROUS THAN MOST OF THE OTHER CREATURES, THOUGH...
...INCLUDING THIS ONE, WHICH IS CON-STANTLY BEING FOOLED BY ITS OWN REFLECTION.

I'D NEVER PART WITH THIS PAIR OF METAL-EATERS, THOUGH... IF ONLY BECAUSE KRYPTONITE IS A RARE DELICACY TO THEM!

FURRED FROG... BEAKED CAT... ANIMAL PLANT... I'VE HAD TO MAKE CERTAIN ALL OF THEM WERE GERM-FREE, IN CASE THEY EVER GOT LOOSE HERE ON EARTH!
AND NONE OF THEM IS EVER LIKELY TO CAUSE AN EXPLOSION BIG ENOUGH TO SPLIT THE PLANET INTO PIECES.
THEN--WHAT IS GOING TO DO IT??

OUBTLESS NOTHING IN MY ARCHIVES ROOM, WHICH ONTAINS TAPES ON ALL KNOWN PLANETS.
THEN, I'D BETTER MOVE ON TO--

GREAT KRYPTON! NOW WHAT?
THE MONITORS HERE--PICKING UP SOME SORT OF DISTRESS SIGNAL-- FROM DEEP SPACE!
BLIP! BLIP! BLIP!

THERE'S THE PROBLEM-- AN ALIEN FREIGHTER OF SOME KIND, ABOUT TO BE DEVOURED BY A SIRIAN STAR-SUCKER!
WITH ONLY TWENTY MINUTES LEFT, AND COUNTING, I DON'T DARE STREAK OFF TO SAVE IT-- AND YET--!
HEY NOW! THERE'S MY IDEA OF A BUDDY-- EVEN IF HE DOESN'T KNOW IT!
GOOD OLD GREEN LANTERN! I KEEP FORGETTING THIS IS HIS SECTOR OF SPACE TO GUARD, AS WELL AS MINE!
I'M OFF THE HOOK!
YET, EVEN AS HE SPEAKS THE WORDS, THE MAN OF STEEL KNOWS HE LIES.
AND THAT 'INTERNAL CLOCK' OF HIS GOES RIGHT ON TICKING...!
37

MEANWHILE, IN A CERTAIN SUBTERRANEAN HIDE-OUT, THOUSANDS OF MILES AWAY...
DOMINUS, DON'T YOU THINK MAYBE WE SHOULD CHECK OUT THAT SO-CALLED MULTI-VERSAL TRANSPORTER OF YOURS?--
--YOU KNOW, THE GIZMO THAT'S GONNA ZAP US TO ANOTHER DIMENSION A SPLIT-SECOND BEFORE THE EARTH GOES BLOOEY?
SURELY, ROGER, YOU'RE NOT STILL HARPING ON THAT!
AFTER ALL, AM I NOT IN THE SAME MORTAL PERIL AS YOU?
OH, SURE--uh, I MEAN--I DON'T KNOW, DOMINUS!
I MEAN--IN AL THE MONTHS I'VE BEEN ASSISTING YOU--I'VE NEVER EVEN SEEN YOUR FACE
Ah, NOW I SEE THE FETID FEAR THAT SPURS YOUR OUTBURST! HA HA HA HA
YOU THINK I MAY BE--A MERE ROBOT--
--AND THAT THE REAL DESTROYER OF THIS EARTH MAY BE LAUGHING UP HIS SLEEVE ALREADY IN ANOTHER DIMENSION!
WELL, sir, NOT EXACTLY--BUT I JUST THOUGHT MAYBE--I MEAN, IF I KNEW WHO I WAS WORKIN' FOR--!
THAT YOU SHALL KNOW AFTER THE CATACLYSM--
--AND NOT BEFORE!
REST ASSURED, ROGER--THIS FOOLPROOF ESCAPE VEHICLE OF MINE WILL DO ITS WORK--
--AS FLAW-LESSLY AS I HAVE DONE MINE!

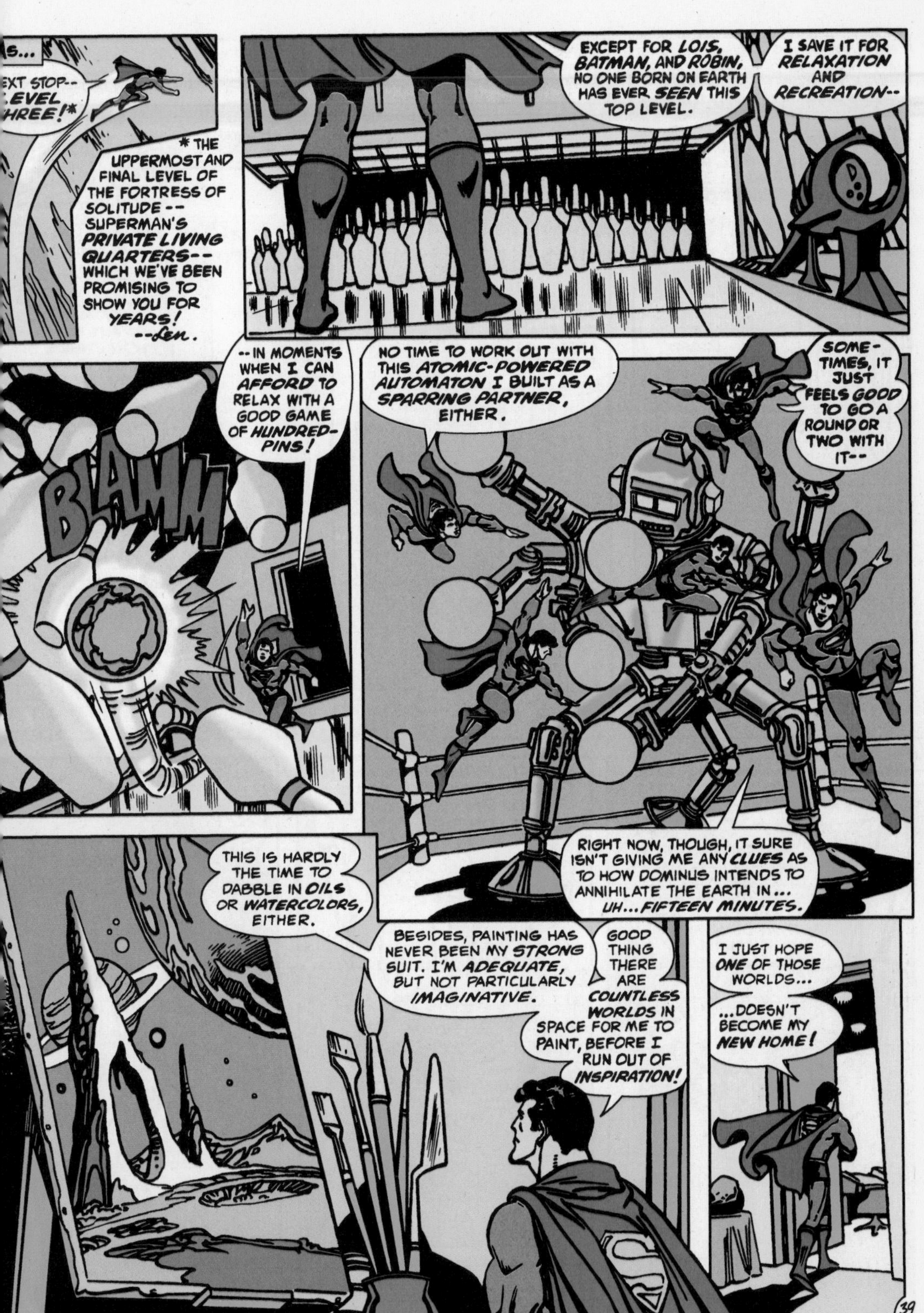

...EXT STOP--
...EVEL
...HREE!*
* THE UPPERMOST AND FINAL LEVEL OF THE FORTRESS OF SOLITUDE -- SUPERMAN'S PRIVATE LIVING QUARTERS-- WHICH WE'VE BEEN PROMISING TO SHOW YOU FOR YEARS! --Len.
EXCEPT FOR LOIS, BATMAN, AND ROBIN, NO ONE BORN ON EARTH HAS EVER SEEN THIS TOP LEVEL.
I SAVE IT FOR RELAXATION AND RECREATION--
--IN MOMENTS WHEN I CAN AFFORD TO RELAX WITH A GOOD GAME OF HUNDRED-PINS!
BLAMM
NO TIME TO WORK OUT WITH THIS ATOMIC-POWERED AUTOMATON I BUILT AS A SPARRING PARTNER, EITHER.
SOME-TIMES, IT JUST FEELS GOOD TO GO A ROUND OR TWO WITH IT--
RIGHT NOW, THOUGH, IT SURE ISN'T GIVING ME ANY CLUES AS TO HOW DOMINUS INTENDS TO ANNIHILATE THE EARTH IN... UH... FIFTEEN MINUTES.
THIS IS HARDLY THE TIME TO DABBLE IN OILS OR WATERCOLORS, EITHER.
BESIDES, PAINTING HAS NEVER BEEN MY STRONG SUIT. I'M ADEQUATE, BUT NOT PARTICULARLY IMAGINATIVE.
GOOD THING THERE ARE COUNTLESS WORLDS IN SPACE FOR ME TO PAINT, BEFORE I RUN OUT OF INSPIRATION!
I JUST HOPE ONE OF THOSE WORLDS...
...DOESN'T BECOME MY NEW HOME!
39

GOT TO GATHER MY THOUGHTS-- CLEAR THE COB-WEBS AWAY, SOMEHOW!
SO MANY WAYS THE WORLD COULD END-- SO LITTLE TIME FOR ME TO FIGURE OUT WHICH ONE IT'LL BE!
DIARY
Hmmm... MY DIARY!

MAYBE WRITING A SHORT ENTRY IN MY NATIVE KRYPTONESE LANGUAGE WILL CALM ME... LET ME THINK MORE CLEARLY.
DIARY
I USED TO ETCH THE WORDS INTO ITS METALLIC PAGES WITH MY BARE FINGERS...

...BUT NOW, I HAVE ONLY TO TOUCH THIS PLATE, AND IT TRANSCRIBES MY THOUGHTS...
...INCLUDING, BLAST IT, THE VERY ONE'S I JUST HAD!
GUESS I'M TOO AGITATED TO DO ANY WRITING NOW-- WHILE THE SECONDS TICK AWAY THE EARTH'S LAST QUARTER-HOUR!

WHAT'S WRONG WITH ME? WHY CAN'T I FIGURE OUT DOMINUS' MADDENING PUZZLE? WHY--?
WAIT A MINUTE! IF DOMINUS IS SOMEONE IN MY PAST, AS I SUSPECT--MAYBE A QUICK LOOK THROUGH MY DIARY WILL--

NO GO! I RE-READ IT COVER TO COVER IN LESS TIME THAN IT TOOK TO THINK OF DOING--
--BUT I'M AS MUCH IN THE DARK AS EVER!
I'M GETTING HYPER-TENSE... NOT THAT THAT SHOULD BE ANY SURPRISE TO ME, AT THIS POINT.

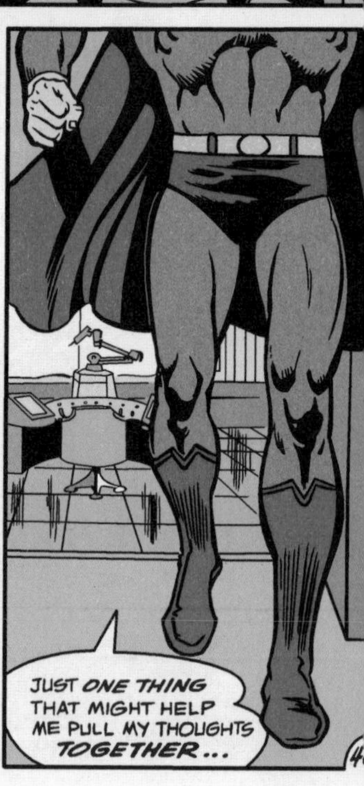
JUST ONE THING THAT MIGHT HELP ME PULL MY THOUGHTS TOGETHER...

...A FAST TROT THROUGH MY FRIENDSHIP EXHIBITS, TO REMIND ME OF THE PEOPLE WHOSE LIVES I'M TRYING TO SAVE:
THE VERY SPECIAL ONE I'VE BUILT TO HOUSE IMAGES OF LOIS LANE...
LOCK OF LOIS' HAIR

...NEXT, THE ONES DEDICATED TO JIMMY OLSEN, ACE REPORTER...

...AND TO PERRY WHITE, GREATEST EDITOR THE DAILY PLANET OR ANY OTHER NEWSPAPER EVER HAD!

I'VE EVEN ERECTED ONE SPOTLIGHTING CLARK KENT...
...JUST IN CASE I BRING SOMEBODY TO THIS LEVEL WHO DOESN'T KNOW MY SECRET IDENTITY.
CLARK KENT'S FAMOUS SCOOPS

HERE'S THE SUPERGIRL EXHIBIT.
OF COURSE, SHE MIGHT SURVIVE... THE SAME AS I MIGHT...

..AND SO MIGHT WONDER WOMAN, THOUGH I DOUBT IF SHE'D EVER DESERT HER FRIENDS AND FAMILY ON PARADISE ISLAND.
NEXT, THE EXHIBIT DEDICATED TO MY FRIEND AND MOST RESPECTED COL-LEAGUE AGAINST EVIL--

--THE BATMAN!
Hmmm...MAYBE TOMORROW I OUGHT TO BUILD AN EXHIBIT TO MY NEW FRIEND CAPTAIN MARVEL, AS WELL--
THE BAD PENNY
--IF THERE IS A TOMORROW!
41

I'VE GOT A TABLEAU DEPICTING MY PARENTS, AS WELL--

--BOTH SETS OF THEM--

--AND ONE OF KRYPTO, WHO WAS MY PET WHEN I WAS SUPERBOY.

THIS SPECIAL GROUPING--OF MY COSTUMED FRIENDS, NEXT TO THEIR TRUE IDENTITIES--WAS ONCE SET TO EXPLODE IF THE FORTRESS WERE ENTERED BY UNAUTHORIZED PERSONS.
NOW, THOUGH, I'VE REDESIGNED IT SIMPLY--
--TO VIBRATE THE WHOLE THING INTO HYPERSPACE TILL THEY LEAVE.

THEN, A SOBERING REALIZATION:
IT--DIDN'T WORK! I'D HOPED TO EASE MY MIND--BY LOOKING AT THOSE IMAGES OF THE PEOPLE I LOVE--
--BUT SEEING THOSE EXHIBITS--JUST MADE IT WORSE--

--JUST BROUGHT HOME TO ME HOW MUCH I'LL BE LOSING IF THE EARTH IS DESTROYED--
SLAM!
--EVEN IF I SURVIVE!

HEAR ME, DOMINUS--IF YOU'RE LISTENING OUT THERE SOMEWHERE
WHY DON'T YOU COME OUT IN THE OPEN--AND FIGHT ME LIKE A MAN!
BUT THERE IS NO ANSWER.
SOMEHOW, SUPERMAN HADN'T REALLY THOUGH THERE WOULD BE.

WELL, ROGER? HOW DO YOU LIKE IT?
OUR LITTLE HOME AWAY FROM HOLOCAUST, WHICH WILL TAKE US TO ANOTHER, ONLY SLIGHTLY LESSER EARTH--
--WHERE THE MAN OF STEEL IS ONLY A CREATURE OF COMIC BOOKS, TV SHOWS, MOVIE SCREENS, AND VIDEO GAMES!
I'LL MISS HIM--AT LEAST FOR A TIME--BUT I'M SURE I'LL FIND OTHER WAYS OF AMUSING MYSELF--
--PROBABLY BY CONQUERING THAT WORLD, OR ELSE DESTROYING IT, TOO!
uh--ARE YOU SURE SUPERMAN WON'T FIGURE OUT A WAY TO STOP THE EARTH FROM BLOWING?
POSITIVE, ROGER.
OH, HE COULD FIGURE IT OUT, I SUPPOSE--
IF HE LIGHTED ON JUST THE RIGHT CLUE, OUT OF SO MANY!
BUT HE WON'T--
--BECAUSE THAT CLUE IS "HIDDEN", SO TO SPEAK, IN THE BEST POSSIBLE PLACE!
AND, er--WHERE'S THAT, DOMINUS?
WHY, RIGHT UNDER HIS NOSE, ROGER--RIGHT UNDER HIS VERY NOSE!
HAVEN'T YOU EVER READ EDGAR ALLAN POE'S "THE PURLOINED LETTER"?
Hmmm... ONLY TEN MINUTES LEFT!
IT WON'T BE LONG NOW..!
43

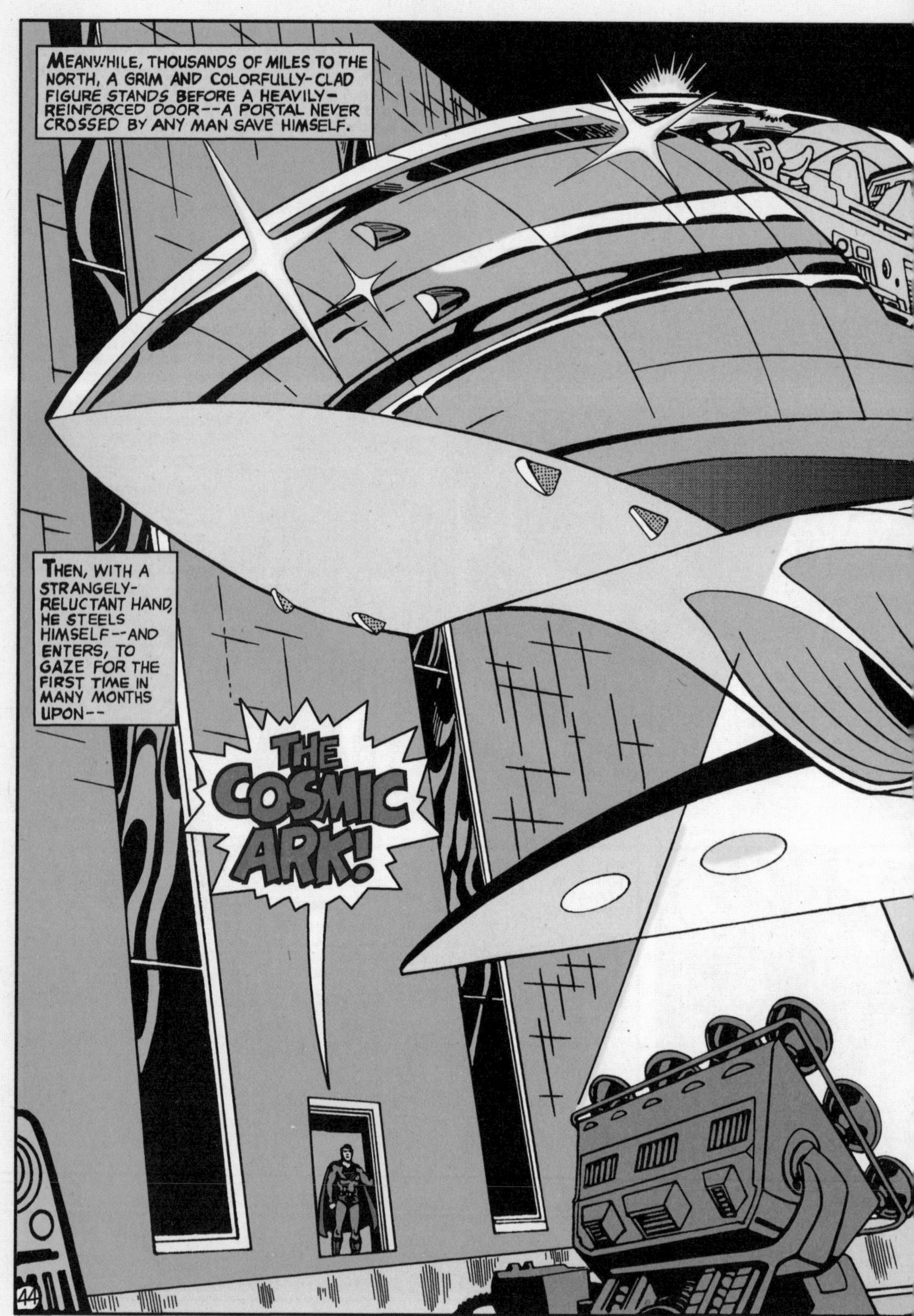
MEANWHILE, THOUSANDS OF MILES TO THE NORTH, A GRIM AND COLORFULLY-CLAD FIGURE STANDS BEFORE A HEAVILY-REINFORCED DOOR--A PORTAL NEVER CROSSED BY ANY MAN SAVE HIMSELF.
THEN, WITH A STRANGELY-RELUCTANT HAND, HE STEELS HIMSELF--AND ENTERS, TO GAZE FOR THE FIRST TIME IN MANY MONTHS UPON--
THE COSMIC ARK!
44

IT SHINES ALMOST LIKE A STAR--BUT IT WAS THE EARTH I WAS THINKING OF WHEN I BUILT IT, NOT LONG AGO.
STRANGE! AT THAT TIME, I HAD A SCENARIO ALL WORKED OUT IN MY MIND--A SCENARIO OF WORLDWIDE DISASTER WHICH MIGHT JUST BE COMING TRUE!
MY SPACE-HOPPING HAS TAUGHT ME JUST HOW FRAGILE THE LIFE OF THE EARTH IS--EVEN WITHOUT MAN'S OWN INHUMANITY TO MAN THROWN IN FOR GOOD MEASURE.
I KNEW THERE WAS ALWAYS THE POSSIBILITY THAT, ONE DAY, A CATASTROPHE WHICH EVEN I COULDN'T STAVE OFF MIGHT THREATEN THE PLANET...
...AND I WANTED TO BE PREPARED FOR IT.
I LIVED THE WHOLE THING IN MY MIND...
45

"...EVEN ASSUMED, HOPING AGAINST HOPE, I'D HAVE TIME TO REACH LOIS, JIMMY, AND PERRY BEFORE THE END CAME.
"WITH LUCK, KARA AND I MIGHT BE ABLE TO GATHER UP A COUPLS OF DOZEN PEOPLE--ALL THE SHIP WILL HOLD--
"--AND ESCAPE THE DOOMED EARTH'S GRAVITATIONAL PULL BEFORE IT EXPLODED.
"FUNNY HOW IT'S ALWAYS AN EXPLOSION YOU THINK OF--
"--THE WORLD ENDING WITH A BANG, NOT A WHIMPER.
"A SMALL HANDFUL OF HUMANITY WOULD SURVIVE, THEN--STRUGGLING TO BUILD NEW LIVES, A NEW CIVILIZATION ON ANOTHER PLANET, IN ANOTHER STAR SYSTEM.
"NO NEED FOR DISGUISES OR SECRET IDENTITIES THERE--ONLY FOR HARD WORK--COMPANSHIP--AND LOVE.
"IT WOULD BE A BRAVE NEW WORLD, I KNOW... BUT IT WOULDN'T BE A VERY HAPPY ONE...
"...NOT FOR A VERY LONG TIME.

NOW, SUPERMAN ENTERS THE FINAL DOORWAY IN THIS ARCTIC CITADEL, TO FIND HIMSELF IN WHAT MAY BE, TO SOME, THE MOST UNEXPECTED CHAMBER OF ALL:
HIS LIVING ROOM.
I'VE NEVER BROUGHT ANYONE HERE IN ALL THE YEARS SINCE I BUILT THE FORTRESS OF SOLITUDE--NOT EVEN LOIS OR BATMAN...
AND NOW I MAY NEVER DO SO.
12:55:74
MY ATOMIC CLOCK SAYS--12:55! SINCE I DESTROYED THE METEOR AT PRECISELY NOON--
--THAT GIVES ME JUST SEVEN MINUTES TO THINK OF SOMETHING.
WELL, I'VE GONE OVER THE FORTRESS FROM A TO Z.
HERE'S WHERE EITHER I PUT IT ALL TOGETHER AND COME UP WITH THE ANSWER--OR--
THE WORDS HOVER, UNSPOKEN, IN THE AIR... TOO PAINFUL TO UTTER AGAIN.
AND, BECAUSE THERE IS NOURISHMENT OF MANY KINDS IN SIMPLE ACTIONS...
...HIS MIND-BOGGLING COMPUTERS ALMOST INSTANTLY MIX HIM...
...A CHOCOLATE SHAKE!
TO SOME, THE ACTION MAY APPEAR FRIVOLOUS...
...EVEN THAT OF A MAN DRIVEN MAD BY FOREKNOWLEDGE OF IMPENDING CALAMITY.
SUPERMAN KNOWS, HOWEVER, THAT HIS MIND CAN USE A FEW SECONDS OF UNRAVELING...
47

AND, AFTER ALL, WHEN ONE HAS SUPER-SENSES...
...EVEN VIDEO-TAPES CAN BE ALTERED TO UNREEL THEIR CONTENTS AT FANTASTIC SPEED...
...A SPEED SO GREAT THAT BOTH SIGHT AND SOUND WOULD BE UTTERLY UNINTELLIGIBLE TO ANY WATCHING EARTHLING...
...WHILE THE SON OF JOR-EL CAN WATCH LITERALLY DOZENS OF SUCH FILMS OR TV PROGRAMS AT ONCE.
HE'S SEEN THEM ALL BEFORE OF COURSE... KNOWS THEIR WORDS AND IMAGES BY HEART.
BUT MERELY REMEMBERING... ISN'T EVERYTHING.
HE WONDERS... IS HE VIEWING THEM ALL FOR THE LAST TIME?
PRECIOUS MINUTES TICK BY, NOT AS UNNOTICED AS THEY APPEAR TO BE.
THEN, HE SCANS THE BOOKS WHICH LINE HIS SHELVES--HIS FEW HUNDRED FAVORITES, OUT OF ALL THE UNTOLD THOUSANDS HE HAS ACCESS TO.
WILL THESE, TOO, PASS FOREVER OUT OF EXISTENCE...
KLIK!
...EXACTLY ONE MINUTE HENCE?
12:58:17
12:59:17
NOTHING IS COMING TO MIND--
--NOTHING!
FOR THE FIRST TIME IN MY LIFE--I'M PARALYZED!
CAN'T EVEN BRING MYSELF TO USE MY COSMIC ARK--
--TO CHOOSE A HANDFUL TO SURVIVE, OUT OF EARTH'S BILLIONS!
THERE MUST BE A CLUE--AT LEAST A STARTING POINT TH
WAIT! MAYBE THAT'S THE MISTAKE I'VE BEEN MAKING ALL ALONG!
GOT TO THINK--THINK!

I'VE BEEN ASSUMING IT WOULD BE JUST ONE THING WHICH WOULD SOMEHOW DESTROY MY FORTRESS--AND THE WORLD.
AT THE MOST, I THOUGHT IT MIGHT BE TWO OR THREE THINGS-- A VERY LIMITED CHAIN OF EVENTS-- WHICH WOULD CAUSE THAT EARTH-DESTROYING EXPLOSION.
BUT--IT MIGHT NOT BE THAT WAY AT ALL!
LUTHOR
WHAT IF THE ANSWER REALLY INVOLVES SEVERAL OBJECTS WITHIN THE FORTRESS-- OR MANY OF THEM--EVEN MOST OF THEM--
--SOME KIND OF FREAK ACCIDENT THAT WOULDN'T HAPPEN MORE THAN ONCE IN A MILLION LIFETIMES-- BUT IS STILL A REMOTE POSSIBILITY--
--LIKE THE LIGHTNING BOLT THAT EVERY ODDS-MAKER IN THE UNIVERSE WOULD BET WON'T STRIKE YOU--BUT STILL MIGHT!
MAYBE SOME COMBINATION OF THINGS--OF EVENTS-- IS ABOUT TO CAUSE THE FINAL BLOW-UP I SAW!
49

ONLY SECONDS LEFT--
--AND SO MANY POSSIBILITIES-- SO MANY COMBINATIONS OF EVENTS!
LUCKILY, THIS PANEL WILL TURN MY THOUGHTS INTO IMAGES--JUST AS THE ONE NEAR MY DIARY TURNS THEM INTO WORDS.
I CAN EXAMINE ANY NUMBER OF COMPLICATED, CAUSE-AND-EFFECT CHAINS, AS FAST AS I CAN THINK OF THEM--
--AND THAT'S PRETTY FAST!
A TOUCH OF AN ANXIOUS HAND...
...AND A LARGER SCREEN DROPS DOW TO COVER THE MANY SMALLER ONES.

NOW, SUPERMAN SEES AGAIN, IN HIS MIND'S-EYE WRIT LARGER, THAT SOUL-SEARING INSTANT WHEN HE SMASHED THE METEOR PULLED EARTHWARD BY THE ELECTRO-MAGNETIC POWER OF THE MYSTERIOUS DOMINUS...
THIS MUST BE WHERE IT ALL BEGAN! IT HAS TO BE!
IN A MATTER OF INSTANTS, COUNTLESS MORE IMAGINARY "SCENARIOS" FLASH UPON THE FAST-FLICKERING SCREEN.

THIS IS ONE OF THEM.
THERE I AM--STREAKING BACK TOWARD MY FORTRESS AFTERWARD.
BUT WHAT IF, WHEN I DESTROYED THE METEOR, I BECAME COATED WITH SOME ALIEN MICRO-ORGANISMS, OF A NEW AND UNKNOWN KIND--

--A TYPE WHICH, INSTEAD OF BEING KILLED BY MY BLOW-TORCH SHOWER--

"--WERE ACTIVATED BY IT INSTEAD!
"SURE! IF THAT HAPPENED, IT CREATES MANY NEW POSSIBILITIES--

"--ONE OF WHICH IS THAT, AS I TOURED THE FORTRESS, THOSE MICRO-ORGANISMS HAD A DELAYED EFFECT ON MY DANCING PLANT, SAY--TURNING IT YELLOW--

"--THE COLOR FIERCELY HATED BY THE ALIEN BEAST IN THE CAGE NEXT TO IT.
"IF IT GOT ANGRY ENOUGH, THE CREATURE COULD BREAK FREE--

"1300 HOURS IS THE EXACT TIME WHEN MY ANTI-BACTERIAL GAS IS SCHEDULED TO BE AUTOMATICALLY RELEASED INTO THE AIR.

"IT CAN'T BE JUST A CO-INCIDENCE!

"THE GAS WOULD PROBABLY KILL EVEN MICRO-ORGANISMS THAT HAD SURVIVED THE BLOWTORCH SHOWER--AND SINCE THEY'VE NOW BECOME A PART OF THE BEAST--
"--THE RESULTING PAIN MIGHT DRIVE IT MAD!
"IT MIGHT SMASH ITS WAY OUT OF THE ZOO AREA, TO OTHER EXHIBITS--

--INCLUDING THE WEAPONS AREA, FOR INSTANCE!
ZZZZZ
"THE ODDS ARE A MILLION OR MORE TO ONE AGAINST IT HAPPENING--BUT THE RIGHT ONE OF THOSE WEAPONS GOING OFF, MIGHT ACTIVATE THE OTHERS--
"--JUST AS ONE FIRECRACKER, TOSSED IN THE RIGHT SPOT, COULD SET OFF AN ENTIRE FIREWORKS STAND!

YES, THAT COULD START A CHAIN REACTION THAT MIGHT DESTROY THE EARTH--
"--BUT WHAT WOULD STOP ME FROM FINDING SOME WAY TO DE-ACTIVATE THE WEAPONS IN TIME?

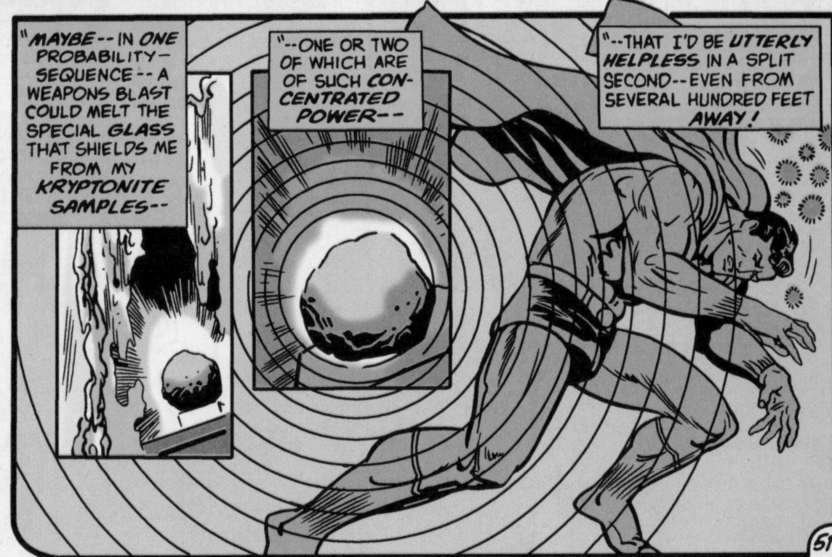

"MAYBE--IN ONE PROBABILITY-SEQUENCE--A WEAPONS BLAST COULD MELT THE SPECIAL GLASS THAT SHIELDS ME FROM MY KRYPTONITE SAMPLES--
"--ONE OR TWO OF WHICH ARE OF SUCH CONCENTRATED POWER--
"--THAT I'D BE UTTERLY HELPLESS IN A SPLIT SECOND--EVEN FROM SEVERAL HUNDRED FEET AWAY!
51

"AND WHILE I STRUGGLED TO RISE, THE VERY *EARTH* AROUND THE FORTRESS WOULD BEGIN TO *SHAKE*--POWERFULLY, *IRRESISTIBLY*--

RRRUMBLE!

"--WITH *REVERBERATIONS* STRONG ENOUGH TO SET EVERY BUILDING ON THE *PLANET* TREMBLING LIKE A LEAF IN A STRONG WIND.

"THAT STILL MIGHT NOT *DESTROY* THE EARTH--BUT--

"*ONE OR TWO* OF MY CONFISCATED SUPER-WEAPONS ARE DEFINITELY CAPABLE OF CAUSING *EXPLOSIONS* GREAT ENOUGH TO DO SO!

"ORDINARILY, NOT EVEN A *THERMONUCLEAR BOMB* COULD SET THEM OFF--

"--BUT JUST THE *'RIGHT'* COMBINATION OF BLASTS FROM A MULTITUDE OF *ALIEN WEAPONS* MIGHT DO IT!

"AND--I JUST THOUGHT OF SOMETHING *ELSE!*--

"IN MY *LAB*, THERE ARE VARIOUS MATERIALS WHICH, IF *COMBINED* SOMEHOW BY COSMIC CHANCE, MIGHT FORM A SUBSTANCE NEARLY *IDENTICAL* TO THE UNSTABLE COMPOUND THAT *DESTROYED KRYPTON!*

"IF THOSE TREMORS *DID* COMBINE THEM--IN A *BILLION-TO-ONE SHOT*--AND IF, SOMEHOW, THAT COMPOUND *MINGLED* WITH THE FORCES IN THE *DISINTEGRATION PIT* BELOW THE FORTRESS--

"--WHICH *ALREADY* CONTAINS SOME RADIOACTIVE KRYPTONIAN ELEMENTS--

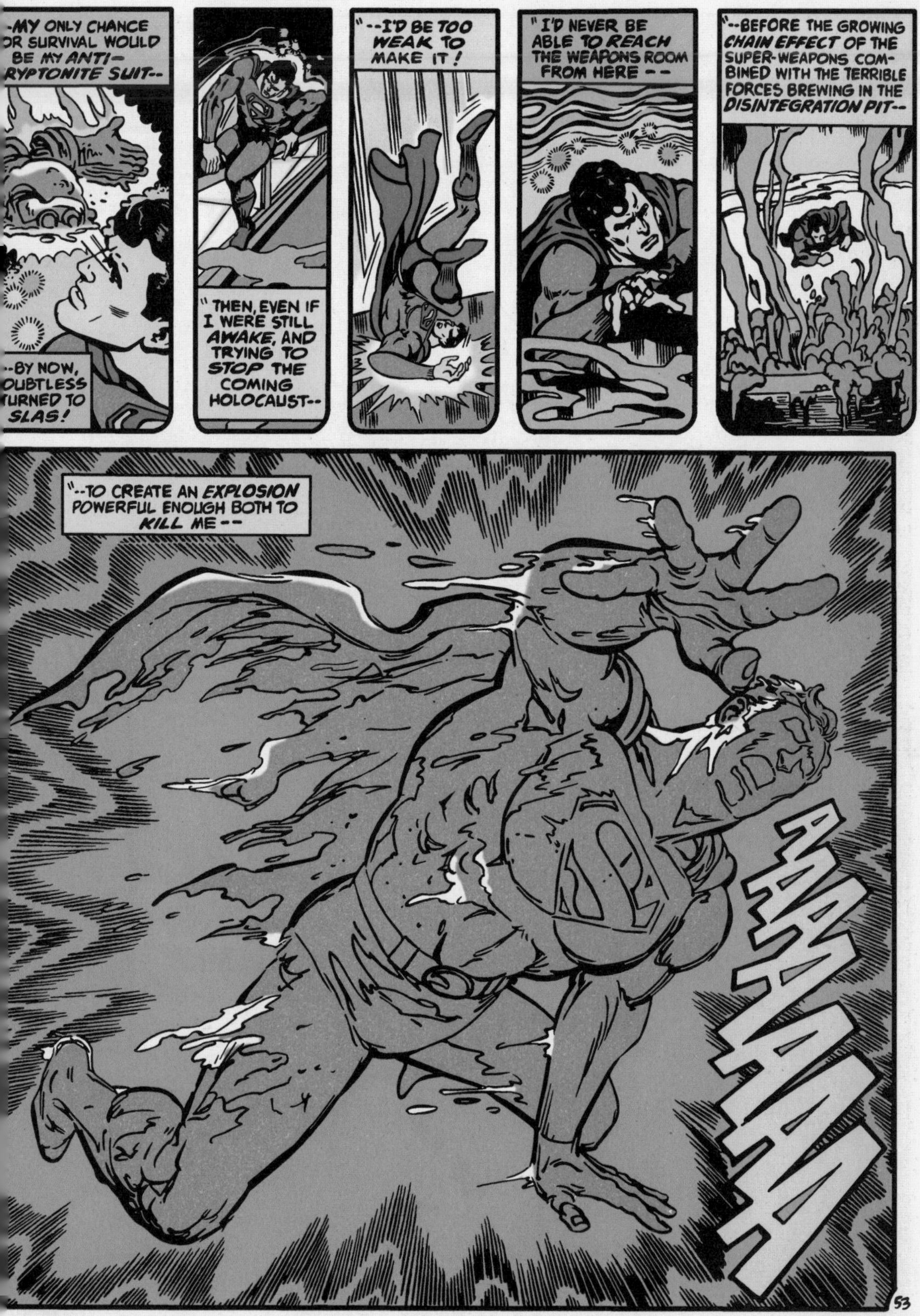

"--TO CREATE AN *EXPLOSION* POWERFUL ENOUGH BOTH TO *KILL ME* --

AAAAHHHH

53

"--AND TO DESTROY THE FORTRESS!
"NO ONE WEAPON--NO, NOT EVE ANY SEVERAL OF THEM--COU GENERATE ENOUGH SHEER, RAW ATOM-DEVOURING POWER TO CRACK THE VERY EARTH, THE W I SAW IT FROM SPACE--
"BUT DOZEN OF THEM, ACTING TOGETHE ON THE WH OF SOME PERVERS FATE--
54

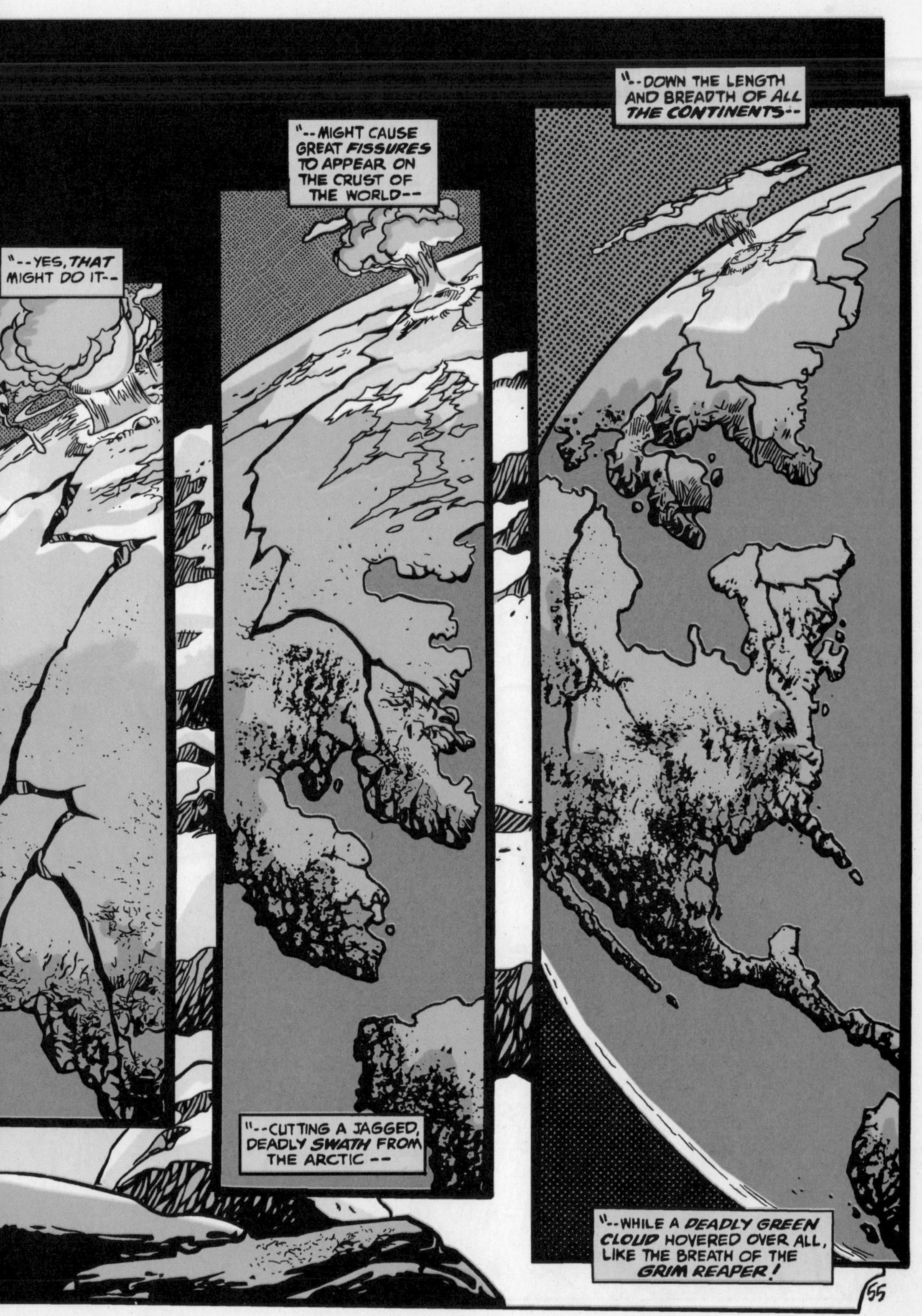
"--YES, THAT MIGHT DO IT--
"--MIGHT CAUSE GREAT FISSURES TO APPEAR ON THE CRUST OF THE WORLD--
"--CUTTING A JAGGED, DEADLY SWATH FROM THE ARCTIC --
"--DOWN THE LENGTH AND BREADTH OF ALL THE CONTINENTS--
"--WHILE A DEADLY GREEN CLOUD HOVERED OVER ALL, LIKE THE BREATH OF THE GRIM REAPER!
55

"AND WHERE, ONLY MOMENTS BEFORE, GREAT SKY-SCRAPERS HAD TOPPLED LIKE CHILDREN'S SAND-CASTLES--
"--WHILE ALL THE EARTH'S MULTITUDES HAD TREMBLED LIKE ANTS IN THE HAND OF A VENGEFUL GOLIATH--
RRRRRUM
56

"--NOW, EVEN THAT CATASTROPHE WOULD BE FORGOTTEN IN A SINGLE, MIND-OBLITERATING INSTANT--
SAVINGS LOAN
TWA
57

"--SINCE NO ONE ON EARTH WOULD BE ALIVE TO REMEMBER IT!
" IN FACT-- THERE WOULD BE NO EARTH!
58

"NOR WOULD THERE BE ANY SOUND--NOT ONLY IN THE NEAR-VACUUM OF SPACE, BUT EVEN IN THE REMNANTS OF THE PLANET'S FAST-DISSIPATING ATMOSPHERE--
"FOR, HOW CAN EVEN THE MOST DEVASTATING EXPLOSION DEAFEN EARS--WHICH NO LONGER EXIST?"
59

THAT'S ONE WAY THE DISASTER COULD STRIKE AT PRECISELY ONE P.M.-- BUT IT'S NOT THE ONLY WAY! THERE ARE COUNTLESS COMBINATIONS OF EVENTS--AND I KNOW IT!
I'VE GOT TO FIND THE WEAK LINK IN ALL THE SIMILAR COMBINATIONS--BREAK IT-- AND PRAY I'VE FOUND THE RIGHT ONE!
IT'S TOO LATE TO DEAL WITH THE MICRO-ORGANISMS...AND I CAN'T BE SURE ABOUT THE DANCING PLANT!
12:59:52
12:59:53
12:59:54
ALL RIGHT, ROGER! CLIMB ABOARD!
WITHIN SECONDS, THE CHAIN REACTION I SET UP WILL BEGIN-- AND THE WORLD IS IRREVERSIBLY DOOMED!
BUT THERE'S ONE LINK THAT OCCURS IN ALL THE SIMILAR SCENARIOS--
--IF ONLY I CAN REACH IT--IN TIME!
12:59:55
12:59:56
12:59:57
WE BETTER REV UP THE MOTOR THEN, HUH, DOMINUS?
I DON'T NEED TO ACTIVATE THE MOTOR! THAT'S THE BEAUTY OF IT!
IT'S DESIGNED TO BE ACTIVATED BY THE GREAT EARTH TREMORS WHICH WILL PRECEDE THE FINAL EXPLOSION!
THE ANTI-BACTERIAL GAS!
THERE! PLUGGED THE NOZZLES-- SO THEY CAN'T RELEASE THEIR CONTENTS AT H-HOUR!
12:59:58
12:59:59
1:00:00
--SO ALL WE MUST DO IS WAIT, FOR THE PROPER VIBRATIONS TO OCCUR, BY MY CALCULATIONS, AT PRECISELY 1:04:47...
...EARTH'S TOTAL DESTRUCTION AT 1:05:28!
Y-YOU REALLY GOT IT TIMED, DON'T YOU, BOSS?
→ 1:00:01 → 1:00:02 → 1:00:03 → 1:00:04 → 1:00:05 → 1:00:06 → 1:00:07 → 1:00:0
NOTHING TO DO NOW-- BUT WAIT!
MY X-RAY VISION SHOWS THAT ALIEN BEAST GOBBLING DOWN MY DANCING PLANT ALREADY--SO I JUST HOPE I'VE REMOVED THE RIGHT PIECE TO PREVENT A DOMINO EFFECT!
MOMENTS PASS...
...AND EVEN SUPERMAN DOESN'T NOTICE JUST HOW WEAK HIS KNEES HAVE BECOME.
BUT AT LAST...HE THROWS BACK HIS HEAD...
...AND LAUGHS

OMINUS, HOWEVER, DOES NOT.
S 1:06--AND STILL NO EMORS, NO EXPLOSION-- OTHING!
WHAT COULD HAVE GONE WRONG? WHAT??

YOU'LL HAVE PLENTY OF TIME TO WORK ON THOSE CALCULATIONS IN PRISON, DOMINUS!
TH-THAT VOICE! IT CAN'T BE--!

SUPERMAN!
YOU'VE JUST PASSED YOUR EYE TEST, DOMINUS...

AND NOW WE'LL ND OUT JUST HO YOU ARE, IN JST A MINUTE...
...NOT THAT I'M NOT STARTING TO GET A FEW IDEAS ALONG THAT LINE...
WELL? ARE YOU COMING OUT--OR DO I PLAY CAN-OPENER?

ROGER--IT SEEMS YOU MUST PRESS THE START-SWITCH, AFTER ALL!
UH-- YESSIR!
IGNITE

NEXT MOMENT, POWERFUL ENGINES ROAR INTO ACTION--
VROOOM!

--BUT SO DO POWERFUL HANDS--

AND FRANKLY... THERE'S REALLY NO CONTEST.
61

BUT, BECAUSE *WOULD-BE WORLD-DESTROYERS* ARE A NOTABLY *STUBBORN* LOT--

--*THIS* SCENARIO, UNLIKE THE ONE INVOLVING EARTH'S DESTRUCTION MUST BE PLAYED OUT TO THE *BITTER END*--

--WHICH IS NOT LONG IN COMING!
KRASH!

NO! NNOOO! AND I WAS SO CERTAIN OF VICTORY--
--I'M NOT EVEN ARMED WITH MY KRYPTONITE-RAY PISTOL!

SOMEHOW, I DON'T TAKE THAT TO MEAN YOU'RE SURRENDERING?
WHAT DO YOU THINK?

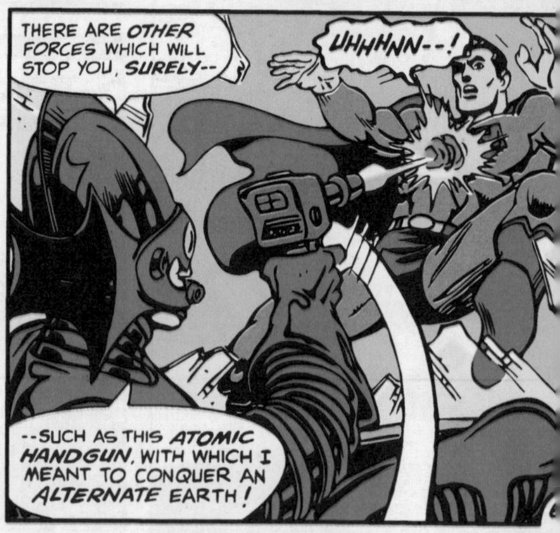

THERE ARE OTHER FORCES WHICH WILL STOP YOU, SURELY--
UHHHNN--!
--SUCH AS THIS ATOMIC HANDGUN, WITH WHICH I MEANT TO CONQUER AN ALTERNATE EARTH!

H! I THOUGHT THE RAYS IT HOOTS--SO SIMILAR TO RYPTONITE IN MANY WAYS--WOULD STOP YOU.
T WOULD TAKE--EVERAL MINUTES OF THOSE AYS--TO ILL ME!
WELL, THANKS TO YOU, I'M NOT GOING ANY-WHERE--
--SO I'VE GOT ALL THE TIME IN THIS WORLD!
WRONG, MASKED MAN! TIME IS EXACTLY WHAT YOU DON'T HAVE! MAYBE YOU CAN HURT ME--
--STOP MY BODY FROM REACHING YOU--
-BUT WHAT ABOUT--SONIC WAVES?
AND NOW, UPERMAN HOUTS--
--LOUDER--
--LOUDER--
--AND LOUDER STILL--UNTIL--
FZZZT!
HEAR THAT, DOMINUS?
T'S THE SOUND OF YOUR ITTLE HOUSE OF ARDS, TUMBLING DOWN AROUND YOUR HELMETED HEAD!
AND HERE COMES THE NEXT NUMBER ON MY OWN PERSONAL HIT PARADE--!
THERE ARE NO LETTERS IN THE ENGLISH ALPHABET TO ADEQUATELY SUGGEST THE SOUND WHICH NOW ERUPTS FROM SUPERMAN'S STAR-BORN THROAT.
SUFFICE IT TO SAY--IT DELIVERS THE GOODS!
63

NOW, JUST IN CASE YOU'VE GOT ANY FURTHER TRICKS UP THOSE ARMORED SLEEVES--
C-CURSE YOU-- SUPERMAN--!
--WE'LL JUST TIE THEM UP WITH A NICE STEEL RIBBON.
AND I'LL BE MIGHTY SURPRISED IF, BEHIND THAT METAL MASK, I DON'T FIND--
--LUTHOR!
YEP!
DO YOU REALLY HATE ME SO MUCH, LUTHOR--THAT YOU'D HAVE DESTROYED THE WORLD TO BE RID OF ME?
CAN YOU DOUBT IT?
ONLY YOU COULD BE BOTH SO BRILLIANT--AND SO EVIL!
WHEN WAS THERE,* I MEMORIZED EVERY LAST INCH OF YOUR FORTRESS OF SOLITUDE.
*ACTION #407. --Len
LATER, IT WAS LARGELY A MATTER OF FIGURING THE PROBABILITIES.
I WORKED HERE--DIRECTLY UNDER THE PRISON--WHILE A HOLOGRAPHIC IMAGE TOOK MY PLACE IN THE CELL FOR HOURS AT A TIME--THE PERFECT COVER.
AH, ROGER! I SEE YOU'VE FOUND MY KRYPTONITE-RAY GUN AMONG THE RUINS!
KILL THIS PIG--NOW!
YOUR ASSISTANT!? I WAS SO BUSY-- HE WAS THE ONE ELEMENT I OVERLOOKED!
WELL, ROGER? WHAT'LL IT BE?
SUPERMAN...
...TAKE THE GUN... PLEASE!
I MUST'VE BEEN INSANE TO FOLLOW DOMINUS-- LUTHOR--THIS LONG.
THIS IS MY WORLD AS MUCH AS ANYBODY'S--
--AND I'D RATHER SERVE TIME HERE THAN RUN OFF TO A NEW ONE!
THEN, I'VE JUST ONE LAST QUESTION, SUPERMAN. HOW DID YOU FIND MY SECRET LAB?
AFTER THE MENACE WAS ENDED, I COULD SWIFTLY RETURN TO SPACE, AND FIGURE OUT WHAT KIND OF RAYS--FROM WHAT POINT ON EARTH--COULD'VE PULLED THAT METEOR HERE IN THE FIRST PLACE!
THE TRAIL OF ELECTRON-MEMORY, AS THEY CALL IT, LED ME STRAIGHT HERE... BENEATH THE STATE PRISON!
YOU MAKE IT SOUND-- SO EASY TO DEFEAT ME!
IT WASN'T REALLY ALL THAT HARD, LUTHOR...
...ONCE I HAD THE TIME...!
--FINIS--

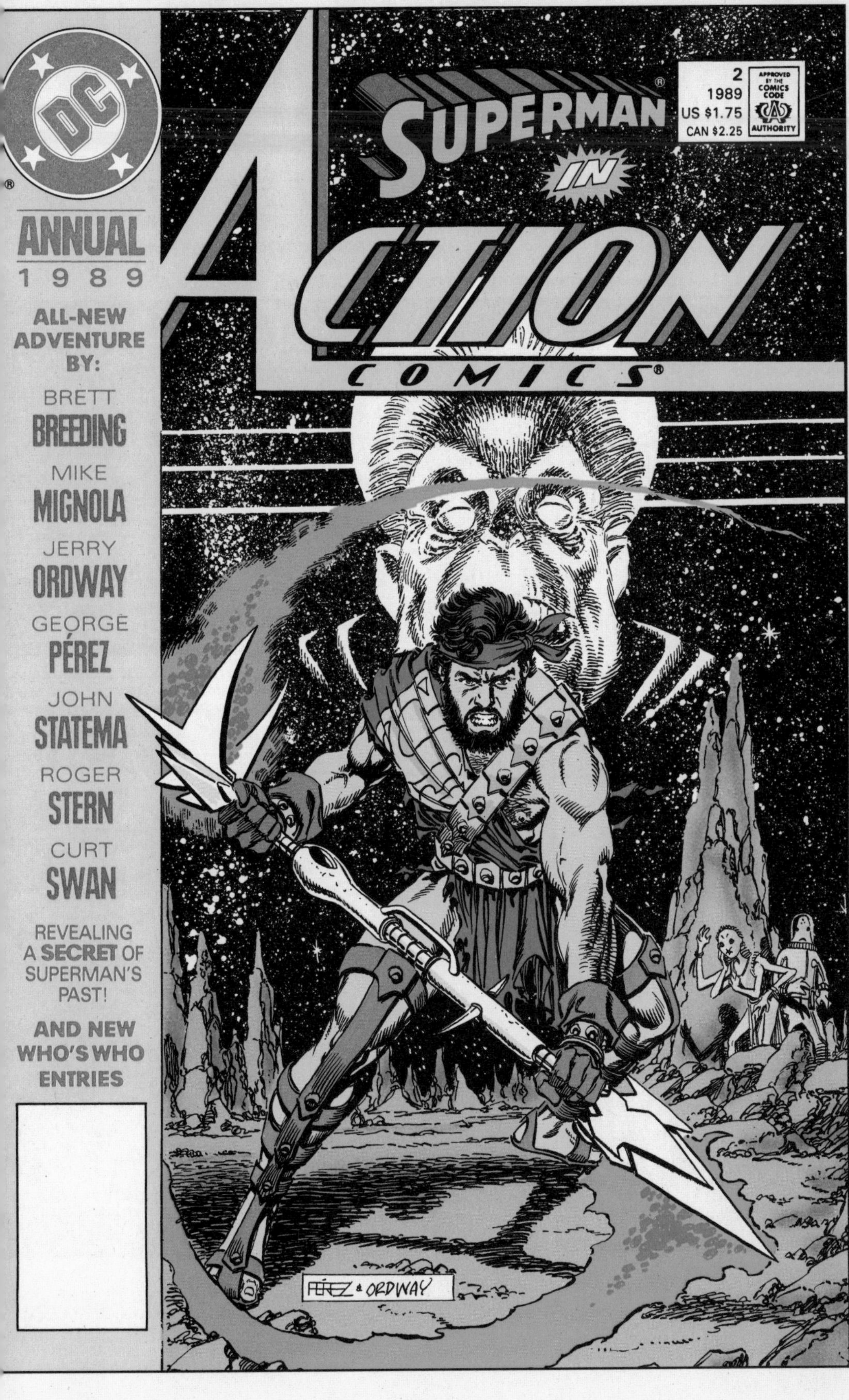

SUPERMAN IN ACTION COMICS

2
1989
US $1.75
CAN $2.25

APPROVED BY THE COMICS CODE AUTHORITY

ANNUAL
1989

ALL-NEW ADVENTURE BY:

BRETT BREEDING
MIKE MIGNOLA
JERRY ORDWAY
GEORGE PÉREZ
JOHN STATEMA
ROGER STERN
CURT SWAN

REVEALING A **SECRET** OF SUPERMAN'S PAST!

AND NEW WHO'S WHO ENTRIES

PÉREZ & ORDWAY

# MEMORIES OF KRYPTON'S PAST

JERRY ORDWAY • JOHN STATEMA
WRITER / PENCILLER — INKER

GEORGE PÉREZ • MIKE MIGNOLA
WRITER / INKER — PENCILLER

ROGER STERN • CURT SWAN • BRETT BREEDING
WRITER — PENCILLER — INKER

BILL OAKLEY letterer • GLENN WHITMORE colorist • RENÉE WITTERSTAETTER asst. editor • MIKE CARLIN el grande honcho

SUPERMAN CREATED BY JERRY SIEGEL AND JOE SHUSTER

FEIST INTERESTS MONGUL, EMPEROR OF WARWORLD.
‹ MAJESTY-- ALLOW ME TO--›
‹ SAVE YOUR ENERGIES FOR THE GAMES, GLADIATOR.›
‹ ADDRESS ME AGAIN AND I'LL HAVE YOUR TONGUE! ›

STILL, FEIST MUST BE KEPT IN IT'S PLACE

‹ BRING HIM FORTH! ›
‹ HE KILLED KAARGL TO GET AT THE BLUE ONE...›
‹SHHH...›

‹ SEE THAT HE IS READY FOR THE FIRST GAME.›

‹ DRAAGA HASN'T HAD A SOLID CHALLENGE FOR MANY CYCLES NOW... ›
‹ TAKE ME BACK TO WARWORLD, LACKEY! ›

THE EXAMINATION BAY...
⟨CELLKEEPER! HELP US WITH MONGUL'S NEW "PET."⟩

⟨I'D LAY ODDS HE'LL NEVER MAKE IT THROUGH THE FIRST CHALLENGE!⟩
FOOSH
⟨THE OTHER GLADIATORS ARE BIGGER, STRONGER...⟩
⟨HE'S USED UP ALL HIS ENERGIES FIGHTING US!⟩
⟨WHERE'S HE FROM?⟩

⟨SLAVE SHIP FOUND HIM IN SPACE, THOUGHT HE WAS DEAD, AND THEY PULLED HIM IN TO SEARCH THE BODY FOR VALUABLES.⟩

⟨SO ONCE INSIDE HE REVIVES AND STARTS FIGHTING,* AND HE'S BEEN AT IT SINCE!⟩

⟨I DON'T SEE WHAT'S SO SPECIAL--⟩

*ADVENTURES OF SUPERMAN #454.

⟨:CLI-ICK!: LIFE FORM IDENTIFIED-- KRYPTONIAN --RACE PREVIOUSLY BELIEVED TO BE EXTINCT-- DATA NOW BEING LOADED INTO MAINFRAME--⟩

⟨HMM-- LAST ONE OF HIS KIND! CROWD'LL LOVE THIS...⟩

⟨TAKE HIM TO A CUBICLE. I'LL HAVE AN ATTENDANT SENT TO PRIME HIM FOR THE START OF THE COMPETITION.⟩

‹RYPTONIAN?! T SEEMS POSSIBLE.›
‹YET, I HAVE NEVER KNOWN THE ANALYZERS TO GIVE A FAULTY READING.›
‹THE CLERIC MUST BE TOLD OF THIS!›
‹ATTENDANT LENTRA!›
‹HOW MAY I BE OF ASSISTANCE, CELLKEEPER?›

‹WE HAVE A NEW GLADIATOR. I PLACE HIM IN YOUR CARE.›
‹I LIVE BUT TO SERVE.›
UT HIM EASE, BUT STRUCT HIM ELL -- HE UST FIGHT ODAY!›

‹A FIRST-TIMER IS BEING SENT DIRECTLY TO THE GAMES?›
‹SUCH IS THE WILL OF MONGUL!›
‹KEEP HIM ALIVE AS LONG AS YOU CAN. HE MAY BE... IMPORTANT.›
I GO NOW... I WILL CONTACT YOU DISCREETLY WITH MORE DETAILS.

‹I MUST PRAY NOW THAT MY ABSENCE GOES UNNOTICED!›

‹IF MONGUL KNEW OF MY ACTIVITIES, I WOULD JOIN THE KRYPTONIAN IN THE GAMES! I HOPE THE CLERIC APPRECIATES THE RISKS I TAKE ON HIS BEHALF.›

THE SHUTTLE-CRUISER SKIMS ALONG THE STAR-LADEN BLACKNESS, AS IT HAS DONE SO MANY TIMES BEFORE.
FOR CELLKEEPERS, SUCH EXCURSIONS ARE ROUTINE. THE INSPECTION AND MAINTENANCE OF THE SATELLITE PRISON ASTEROIDS ARE JUST PART OF THE JOB.
BUT, FOR CELLKEEPER 385, IT HAS BECOME SO MUCH MORE...
...ESPECIALLY TODAY.
⟨385 TO GLADIATOR ATTENDANT LENTRA. RESPOND ON FREQUENCY OPENED. REPLY.⟩
⟨385, IS THAT YOU? IT'S LENTRA.⟩
⟨WHY ARE YOU CALLING ON THIS CHANNEL? IT'S AGAINST REGULATIONS.⟩
⟨I COULDN'T RISK USING THE MONITORED STATIONS.⟩
⟨IF WHAT THEY SAY ABOUT THE RED-C ALIEN IS TRUE, THE OL CLERIC MUST BE INFORMED.⟩
⟨PLEASE, LENTRA, YOU MUST ATTEND THE KRYPTONIAN.⟩
⟨THIS MAY BE THE SIGN WE'VE BEEN PRAYING FOR.⟩
⟨WHAT YOU'VE BEEN PRAYING FOR. I DON'T BELIEVE ANY OF THIS.⟩
⟨BUT DON'T WORRY, 385. I'LL SEE TO THE ALIEN'S
⟨LENTRA! REPLY! LENTRA!⟩

"⟨BLAST! I LOST HER. THE SUB-FREQUENCY IS NOT AS STRONG AS THE OFFICIAL CHANNELS.⟩
"⟨WELL, NO MATTER. LENTRA WILL DO AS I ASK, EVEN IF SHE DOES FEAR MONGUL'S WRATH.⟩
"⟨WE'VE BEEN FRIENDS FOR TOO LONG.⟩
"⟨AH! THERE IT IS!⟩

"⟨DETENTION BLOCK Z.⟩
"⟨THE MOST SEQUESTERED OF ALL THE ISOLATION ASTEROIDS.⟩"

⟨THE PARIAH PENITENTIARY.⟩

IN THE CAVERNS OF THE PRISON PLANET, THE NEW ACQUISITION HAS SLOWLY REGAINED CONSCIOUSNESS.

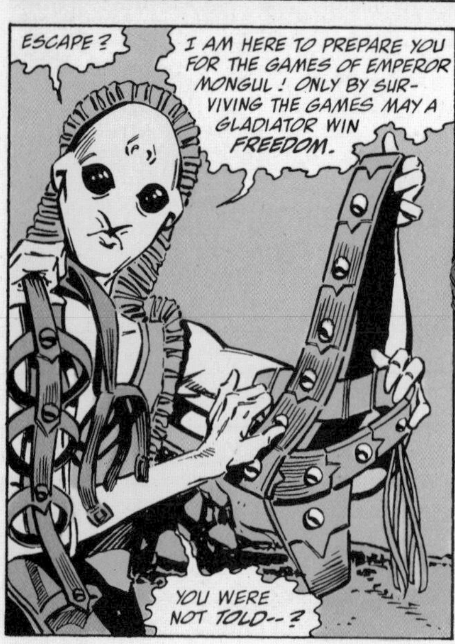

I AM SURE YOU ILL GIVE A GOOD CCOUNTING OF OURSELF! YOU PPEAR QUITE FIT!
I'VE HEARD A DOZEN DIFFERENT LANGUAGES SINCE I WAS BROUGHT HERE... AND DIDN'T UNDERSTAND ONE OF THEM. HOW IS IT THAT WE CAN COMMUNICATE?
I AM A EVEL-THREE ELEPATH.

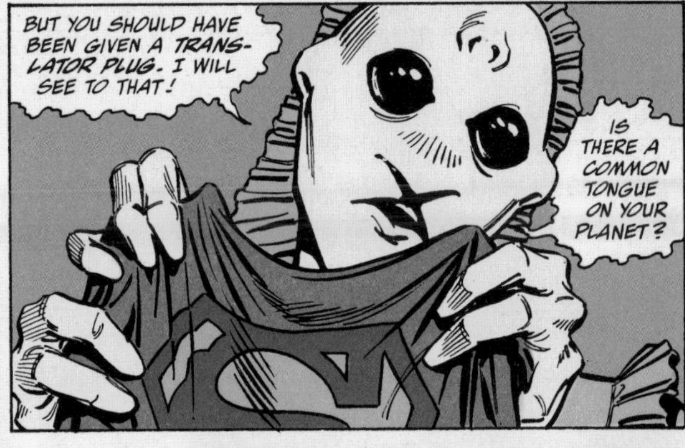
BUT YOU SHOULD HAVE BEEN GIVEN A TRANSLATOR PLUG. I WILL SEE TO THAT!
IS THERE A COMMON TONGUE ON YOUR PLANET?

NO, MY WORLD HAS MANY LANGUAGES.
WHAT IS IT LIKE?

IT'S A BEAUTIFUL PLACE... WE CALL IT SIMPLY "EARTH." BILLIONS OF PEOPLE LIVE THERE, MANY OF THEM CLUSTERED TOGETHER IN GREAT CITIES. MY CITY WAS METROPOLIS.
"YOU ARE THE CHAMPION OF THIS... METROPOLIS?"
"I WAS."
DAILY PLANET
S.T.A.R.
"YOU HAVE FAMILY THERE?"

NO... MANY FRIENDS, THOUGH. MOST OF THEM WORK TO COLLECT THE NEWS OF THE DAY-- FROM ALL OVER THE PLANET-- FOR THE CITIZENS OF METROPOLIS.

"MY FAMILY LIVES ON A FARM, HUNDREDS OF MILES FROM THE CITY. THAT'S WHERE I WAS BORN.
"MY PARENTS ARE HARD-WORKING SMALL-TOWN FOLK... BUT THEY WERE NEVER SMALL-MINDED. THEY ALWAYS ENCOURAGED ME TO THINK BEYOND THE CONFINES OF THE FARM.
"I WONDER WHAT DAY IT IS BACK HOME?

"IF IT'S SUNDAY, I IMAGINE THAT MA AND PA WILL BE SITTING DOWN TO AN EARLY DINNER WITH THE NEW FOSTER CHILD THEY'VE TAKEN IN.
"IF I KNOW MA, SHE'LL HAVE INVITED LANA LANG OVER, TOO. I CAN ALMOST TASTE THE CHICKEN AND DUMPLINGS."

I HOPE THEY'RE ALL WELL. THEY'RE SO VERY FAR AWAY... AND I MISS THEM ALL SO VERY MUCH.
YOUR WORLD SOUNDS SO PLEASANT. WHY DID YOU LEAVE IT?
THAT'S... A LONG STORY.
LET'S JUST SAY I THOUGHT IT BEST FOR ALL CONCERNED THAT I GO OFF-PLANET.

HEY! BRING BACK MY CAPE!!
MA SAID TO WEAR IT... WHEREVER I GO.

EANWHILE, IN
DETENTION
OCK 2...
‹STRANGE. I THOUGHT I'D BE REALLY NERVOUS ABOUT THIS. THE OLD CLERIC USUALLY HAS THE KNACK FOR DIS-COMBOBULATING MY INNARDS.›
‹MAYBE IT'S BECAUSE, FOR ONCE, IT IS I WHO HAVE SOMETHING TO TEACH HIM.›
‹BRRR. THAT FAMILIAR CHILL IN MY MEMBRANES.›
‹HE KNOWS I'M HERE.›

85, WHY DO YOU OME TO BOTHER ME NOW?›
‹I'VE TOLD YOU REPEATEDLY, MY TIME FOR PREACHING IS PAST.›
‹BUT CLERIC, I HAVE SEEN A WONDROUS SIGHT! ONE THAT I MUST SHARE WITH YOU!›

‹I DO NOT CARE. SIGHTS OF WONDER ARE FOR THOSE WHO CARE TO SEE.›
‹I JUST WANT TO BE LEFT ALONE.›

‹HOLY ONE, NO ONE RESPECTS YOUR WISHES MORE THAN I, BUT I CANNOT ALLOW YOU TO DECAY HERE ANY LONGER.›
‹NOT WHEN THE ANSWER TO YOUR PRAYERS AWAITS WITHIN THE DARK RECESSES OF WARWORLD.›

‹YOU SPEAK IN RIDDLES, CELLKEEPER. AND I FIND RIDDLES TIRESOME.›
‹IF YOU HAVE SOMETHING TO SAY, SAY IT.›
‹ELSE, TURN FROM ME, AND RETURN NO MORE.›

‹WITH DUE RESPECT, CLERIC, YOU WOULDN'T BELIEVE MY WORDS.›
‹BUT IF YOU WITNESSED THROUGH MY MIND'S EYES AND SEE WHAT I'VE SEEN...›
‹OH, VERY WELL THEN. IF ONLY TO BE RID--›
‹THERE! SEE IT? THAT READOUT IN THE EXAMINATION BAY.›
‹LIKE THE IMAGES YOU PLANTED IN MY MIND SO LONG AGO.›
‹A KRYPTONIAN!?›
‹NO! IT CAN'T BE!›
‹IT IS A TRICK! A PLOT TO DRIVE ME MAD!›
‹NO KRYPTONIAN CAN STILL BE ALIVE! IT'S IMPOSSIBLE!›
‹THEY'RE DEAD! THEY ARE ALL DEAD!!›

T IS
LMOST
TIME FOR
ATTLE...
HERE. THESE
WILL ENABLE
YOU TO
BREATHE THE
ARENA'S
ATMOSPHERE.
WHAT
DO I
DO
WITH--

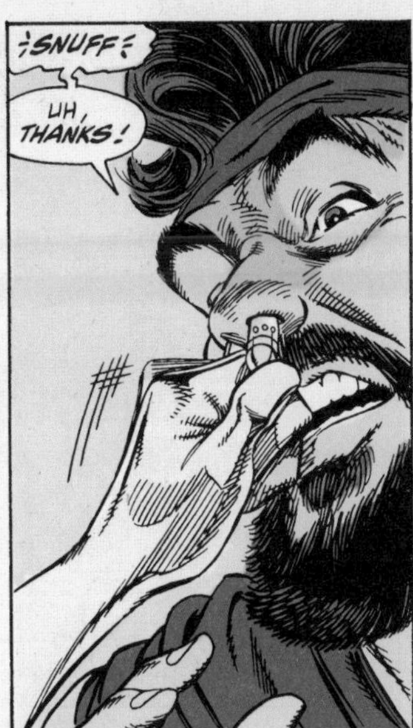
SNUFF
UH,
THANKS!

YOU'VE
BEEN VERY
HELPFUL.
I KNOW I WILL
SEE YOU AGAIN.
THERE IS AN AURA
ABOUT YOU.

THESE
"JUMPS"
ARE A BIT
UNNERV-
ING!
HMM ... A BARREN
TERRAIN. I'D IMAGINED
AN ARENA OF SOME
SORT.
THAT LIGHT UP
AHEAD MUST HERALD
MY OPPONENT'S
ARRIVAL.
"HEAR
ME,
WARRIORS..."

...THE SOLE RULE
OF THIS CONTEST IS
THAT THIS IS TO BE
A FIGHT TO THE
DEATH...
TO THE DEATH!
TO THE DEATH!
ON MY WORD,
LET THE GAMES
BEGIN!

TO THE DEATH? THE CROWD'S BOUND TO BE DIS-APPOINTED...
I WON'T KILL -- ESPECIALLY NOT FOR SPORT!

I HAVE NO DOUBT THAT MY OPPONENT WILL BE AFTER MY BLOOD -- IF HE EVER SHOWS HIS FACE!
I CERTAINLY DIDN'T LEAVE EARTH TO BECOME A GLADIATOR!

IF MY POWERS WERE AT THEIR PEAK, I'D BE LONG GONE-- AWAY FRO--

SSSSSS

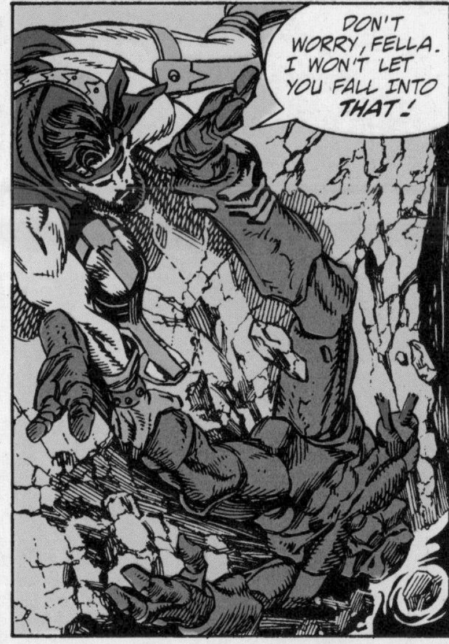
DON'T WORRY, FELLA. I WON'T LET YOU FALL INTO THAT!

‹DEATH! KILL HIM! FOLLOW THE RULES!›

NO! HE'S
FFERED ENOUGH
R YOUR ENTER-
TAINMENT!
THERE WILL BE NO BLOOD ON MY HANDS!
‹YOU HAVE BESTED ME-- NOW KILL ME...›
‹...IT IS THE WAY OF THE GAMES!›

" DON'T CARE!
'M CHANGING
HE RULES!"
‹KILL THEM BOTH!›
‹THIS WEAKNESS WILL DOOM HIM IN THE NEXT CONTEST!›

I'M BACK?!
YOU ARE HERE TO REST UP FOR THE NEXT PHASE.
NEXT PHASE? I WON'T-- CAN'T KILL! THERE'S JUST NO WAY MONGUL CAN FORCE ME!

WHY DO I BOTHER TELLING YOU? EVERYONE HERE JUST DOES WHAT HE TELLS THEM TO!
DO NOT JUDGE US ALL SO HARSHLY-- WE MERELY DO WHAT WE MUST, TO SURVIVE.
PERHAPS IF YOU TELL ME MORE ABOUT YOUR WORLD, IT WILL BE EASIER TO UNDERSTAND YOUR BIAS.

THE ANALYZERS IDENTIFIED YOUR ORIGINS AS KRYPTONIAN, YET YOU CALLED YOUR WORLD "EARTH"-- AND I SENSED NO DECEPTION ON YOUR PART. I AM PUZZLED.
I'M NOT SURPRISED.
I WAS BORN ON EARTH AND LIVED THERE FOR OVER A QUARTER- CENTURY BEFORE I DISCOVERED THAT MY BLOODLINE WAS OF ANOTHER WORLD.
I WAS HOME FOR A VISIT TO MY PARENTS' FARM...

"--WHEN I FIRST LEARNED OF MY NATURAL FATHER..."
MY SON... BE SILENT... AND LEARN!
"HE APPEARED LIKE A GHOST ON THE PRAIRIE, BUT THERE WAS MORE TO HIM THAN JUST LIGHT AND SOUND.

"HE WAS A MANIFESTATION OF... A SORT OF ELECTRO-PSIONIC RECORDING -- A MESSAGE FROM A FATHER I'D NEVER KNOWN, A MAN NAMED JOR-EL.

"IN A MATTER OF SECONDS, MY MIND WAS OVERWHELMEI BY A BURST OF DATA-- A LIFETIME OF MEMORIES FROM THE LONG-DEAD WORLD OF KRYPTON.

JOR-EL, I LEARNED, HAD BEEN A BRILLIANT SCIENTIST... AND PERHAPS THE LAST ROMANTIC ON THAT SAD OLD WORLD..."
WHERE IS THE CHILD?
FOLLOWING YOUR EARLIER INSTRUCTIONS--

--I HAVE PLACED THE MATRIX IN THE THIRD LEVEL LABORATORY, SIRE."
MY... SON...
JOR-EL!! THEN IT IS TRUE...

...YOU REALLY SENT ONE OF YOUR SERVANTS TO REMOVE THE MATRIX FROM THE GESTATION CHAMBERS!
AM I NOT ENTITLED TO DO SO IF I WISH, LARA? I AM THE CHILD'S FATHER. BY KRYPTONIAN LAW, I HAVE THE RIGHT TO REMOVE HIM.
YOU SPEAK OF A LAW THAT HAS NOT BEEN INVOKED FOR CENTURIES, JOR-EL-- WHY DO YOU INVOKE IT NOW? HAS THE TRAGEDY THAT BESETS OUR WORLD ROBBED YOU OF YOUR SANITY?

IS THIS WHY YOU ENDANGER THE LIFE OF OUR UNBORN CHILD?
"ENDANGER?" WHAT I MEAN TO DO WILL NOT ENDANGER HIM, LARA. HE WILL SURVIVE. LONG AFTER ALL OF KRYPTON IS A SHATTERED RUIN, OUR SON WILL SURVIVE!

JOR-EL AND LARA WERE MY GENETIC PARENTS... THEY GAVE ME LIFE.
BUT MY EARTH PARENTS GAVE ME LOVE.

<CLERIC, I DON'T UNDERSTAND. THAT RED-CAPED ALIEN *HAS* TO BE A KRYPTONIAN. THE DATA IN THE MAINFRAME WAS *CONCLUSIVE*.>
<MACHINES ARE NOT INFALLIBLE, 385.>
<THAT LIFEFORM IS A PHYSICAL IMPOSSIBILITY, PARTICULARLY THIS FAR OUT IN SPACE.>

<BEAR WITNESS TO THE IMAGES FROM *MY* MIND'S EYES, CELLKEEPER...>
<...AND YOU WILL SEE **WHY**.>
<BUT CLERIC, I HAVE ALREADY SEEN THESE IMAGES...>
"<BUT NOT **ALL** OF THEM, YOUNG ONE. UNTIL NOW, NO ONE BUT I HAVE SEEN THESE MEMORIES OF KRYPTON PAST.>
"<RETURN WITH ME ONCE MORE TO THOSE FATEFUL DAYS SO LONG AGO.>

"<WHEN MY HOLY MISSION BROUGHT ME TO THAT LUSH, GLORIOUS EMERALD PLANET.>

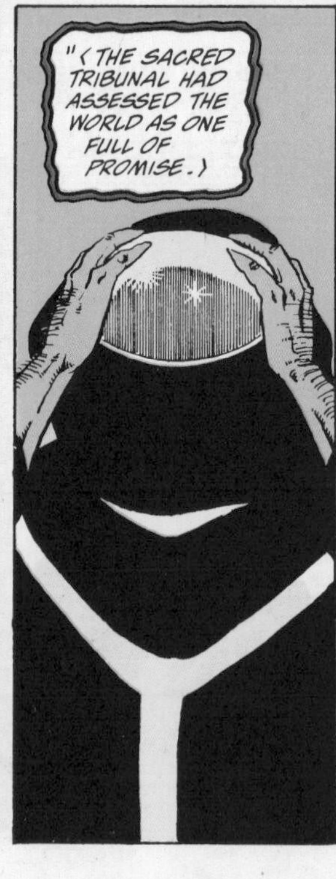
"<THE SACRED TRIBUNAL HAD ASSESSED THE WORLD AS ONE FULL OF PROMISE.>

"<A PROMISE THAT I HAPPILY SOUGHT TO FULFILL.>

"⟨ AMONG ALL THE PRIESTS OF MY ORDER, MY RECORD FOR PROSELYTISM WAS ENVIED. ⟩
"⟨ I HAD BROUGHT MANY IMMIGRANT CONVERTS BACK TO THE HOLY COMMUNE, WHICH BOASTED THE GREATEST INTERPLANETARY DIVERSITY IN THE UNIVERSE. ⟩
"⟨ AS I WATCHED THE ATTENTIVE FACES OF MY KRYPTONIAN AUDIENCE, I COULD SEE HOW MY WORDS STIRRED THEM. ⟩
"⟨ A STATE OF CONFUSION AND UNREST HAD SETTLED ON THE LAND. THEY LOOKED TO ME FOR GUIDANCE. ⟩
"⟨ MY ARRIVAL, I THOUGHT, WAS WELL-TIMED INDEED. ⟩
⟨ THE PRIEST'S WORDS HAVE THE RING OF WISDOM, SEN-M. ⟩
⟨ YES, SYRA. I MUST ADMIT THAT HIS ARGUMENTS AGAINST CLONING ARE QUITE PERSUASIVE. ⟩
⟨ PEOPLE OF KRYPTON! WE MUST PROTEST WITH ALL OUR HEARTS THIS FOULEST OF BLASPHEMIES! ⟩
⟨ THE PURVEYORS OF HEARTLESS SCIENCE ATTEMPT TO USURP THE PRIVILEGE OF THE DIVINE DIETY. ⟩
⟨ YET, WHILE THEY MAY REPLICATE THE BODY, IT IS BUT A HOLLOW SHELL! ⟩
⟨ THEY CANNOT REPLICATE THE SOUL! ⟩
⟨ CLONING IS AN AFFRONT TO ALL CREATION! ⟩
⟨ DO YOU HEAR THAT, FELLOW MEMBERS OF THE SCIENCE COUNCIL? ⟩
⟨ THIS FANATIC IS STIRRING UP INSURRECTION, UNDERMINING SCIENTIFIC PROGRESS. ⟩
⟨ HE MUST BE SILENCED! ⟩

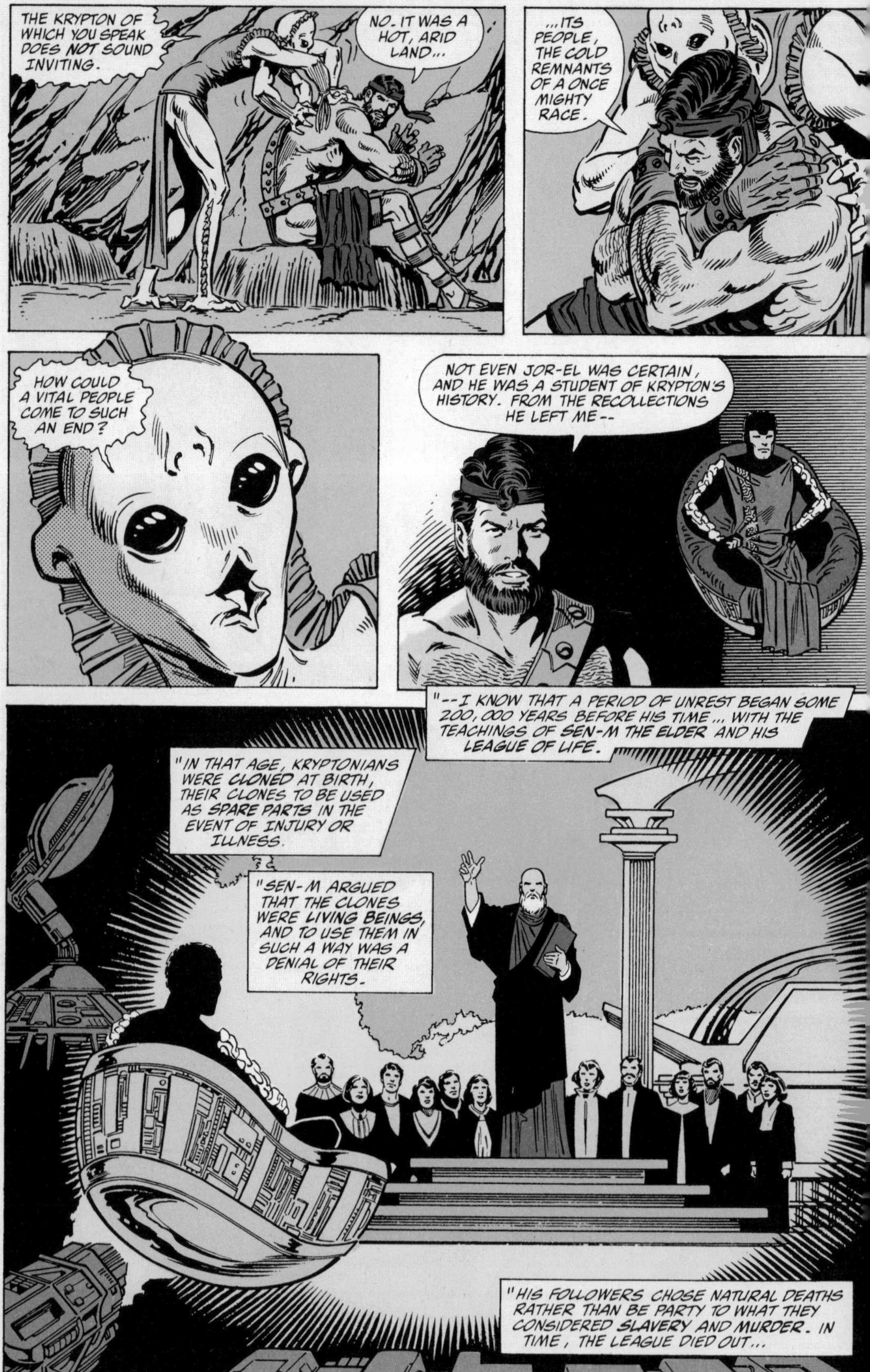

"--I KNOW THAT A PERIOD OF UNREST BEGAN SOME 200,000 YEARS BEFORE HIS TIME... WITH THE TEACHINGS OF SEN-M THE ELDER AND HIS LEAGUE OF LIFE.

"IN THAT AGE, KRYPTONIANS WERE CLONED AT BIRTH, THEIR CLONES TO BE USED AS SPARE PARTS IN THE EVENT OF INJURY OR ILLNESS.

"SEN-M ARGUED THAT THE CLONES WERE LIVING BEINGS, AND TO USE THEM IN SUCH A WAY WAS A DENIAL OF THEIR RIGHTS.

"HIS FOLLOWERS CHOSE NATURAL DEATHS RATHER THAN BE PARTY TO WHAT THEY CONSIDERED SLAVERY AND MURDER. IN TIME, THE LEAGUE DIED OUT...

...BUT THE **DEBATE** OVER THE USE OF CLONES LIVED ON. A **CLONES RIGHTS** MOVEMENT GREW IN POWER... ERUPTING INTO RIOTING AND TERRORISM.

‹GREAT AND EXALTED MONGUL-- IF THE KRYPTONIAN WINS THIS CONTEST...›
‹...HE FIGHTS YOUR CHAMPION, DRAAGA!›
‹DRAAGA HANDILY WON HIS FIRST BOUT, LORD!›

‹I BID YOU TO SPEAK, WARRIOR.›
‹GREAT MONGUL-- I OFFER YOU THE HEAD OF MY VANQUISHED FOE, IN OBSERVANCE OF THE RULE OF THE GAMES...›

‹I DON'T CARE ABOUT THIS ONE-- HIS KIND ARE LEGION...›
‹BRING ME THE HEAD OF THE KRYPTONIAN, SO THAT I MAY FEAST ON HIS EYES-- AND SAVOR THE END OF HIS RACE!›
SLAP!

‹LET THE CONTEST RESUME --THE KRYPTONIAN VERSUS THE MONMOUTH...›

‹I'LL WAGER TEN UNITS ON THE KRYPTON-MAN!›
‹AND I'LL COVER THOSE ODDS...›

"HE DOESN'T STAND A CHANCE AGAINST THE MONMOUTH!"
THIS GUY'S NOT WASTING ANY TIME AT ALL!
RAAAAAAA
WAIT! LISTEN TO ME...

WE DON'T HAVE TO DO THIS! MONGUL DOESN'T OWN US!

ALL OF THE PLAYERS IN THIS "GAME" ARE POWERFUL FIGHTERS...
WE COULD BAND TOGETHER AGAINST MONGUL!

NO! THROUGH COMBAT I EARN RESPECT FOR MY KIND...
SMASH!

GREAT MONGUL GAVE ME THAT CHANCE... URRGH!
MONGUL'S INFLUENCE IS STRONG, IT SEEMS...
I'LL HAVE TO WIN SOME INFLUENCE OF MY OWN, FIGHTING MY WAY!
I THINK MY MICROSCOPIC VISION HAS DETECTED THIS GUY'S ACHILLES' HEEL...

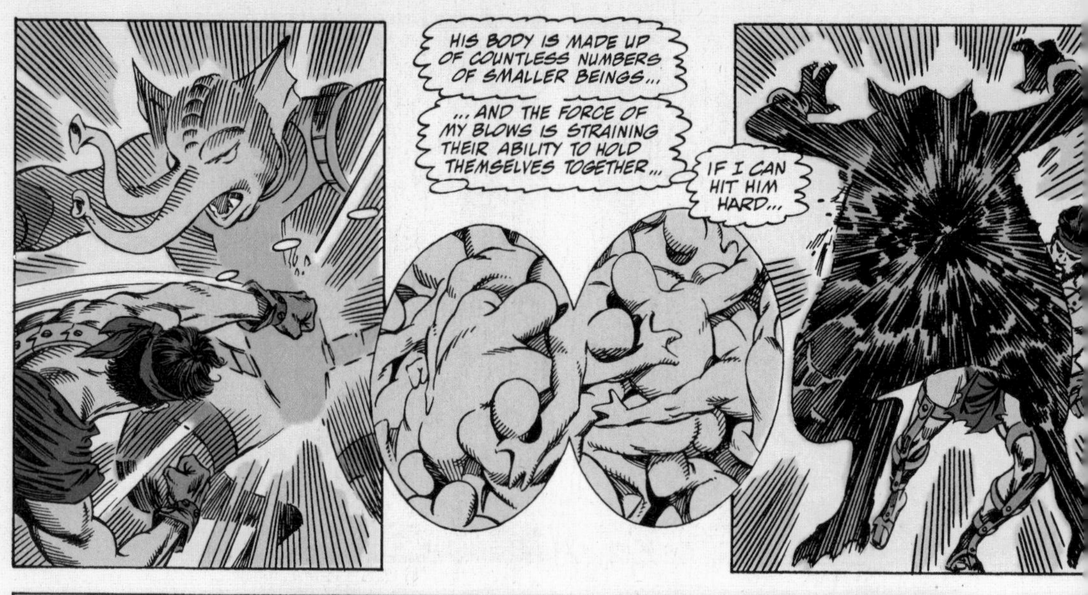
HIS BODY IS MADE UP OF COUNTLESS NUMBERS OF SMALLER BEINGS...
...AND THE FORCE OF MY BLOWS IS STRAINING THEIR ABILITY TO HOLD THEMSELVES TOGETHER...
IF I CAN HIT HIM HARD...

...ENOUGH!
THINK FAST, CLARK!

A BLAST OF WIND SHOULD SPREAD THEM AROUND SO THEY CAN'T RE-COMBINE RIGHT AWAY!
I GUESS THIS MAKES ME THE WINNER. WONDER WHAT CO-- HEY!

...THESE FELLOWS DON'T LOOK TOO HEALTHY--MAYBE THEY CAN'T SUR-VIVE SEPARATELY IN THIS ATMOS-PHERE!

‹AGAIN, THE KRYPTON-MAN DOES NOT KILL!›
‹THE MONMOUTH WOULD HAVE PERISHED, BUT THE KRYPTONIAN IS GATHERING TO-GETHER ITS MANY PARTS!›
‹I STILL WIN THE WAGER!›

‹KNOW THIS --MONGUL WILL NOT LET HIM LIVE, WHEN HE DEFEATS DRAAGA!›

"⟨ CLERIC, I DON'T REMEMBER EVER SEEING THAT STRUCTURE BEFORE. ⟩"
"⟨ BECAUSE I HAD HERETOFORE NEVER SHOWN IT TO YOU. ⟩
"⟨ THERE, CELLKEEPER, IS THE TEMPLE OF THE DIVINE DEITY. ⟩
⟨ IN ITS HEART, WE PRAYED TOGETHER, SAVORING THE BENEFICENT TEACHINGS OF THE HOLY WORD. IT WAS A CAUTIOUS TIME. MY DISCIPLES WERE WELL AWARE OF THE DANGERS FROM WITHOUT. ⟩
"⟨ THE SCIENCE COUNCIL HAD OBTAINED THE SUPPORT OF THE FOLLOWERS OF RAO, THE PLANET'S OFFICIAL, HEATHEN RELIGION. ⟩
"⟨ ALTHOUGH THE RAOIST PRIESTS SHOWED NO HIGH REGARD FOR THE CLONING ABOMINATION, THEY FOUND THE WORDS OF THE DIVINE DEITY TO BE AN EVEN GREATER THREAT. ⟩
"⟨ IN THIS HERETIC ALLIANCE, THE SCIENTISTS INVOKED RAO'S NAME AS THE PROPONENT-- IN FACT, CREATOR-- OF THE CLONING CONCEPT. AMAZING HOW GOD CREATES SCIENTIST-- WHO IN TURN RECREATE GOD. ⟩
"⟨ AS IT WAS ON SO MANY OTHER WORLDS, THE FOLLOWERS OF THE DIVINE DEITY BECAME OUTCASTS, PERSECUTED FOR THEIR BELIEFS. ⟩
"⟨ I KNEW THAT THE TIME OF THE GREAT PROCLAMATION WAS AT HAND. MY MISSION WAS ALMOST COMPLETE. ON THIS DAY I GATHERED THE FAITHFUL TO THE TEMPLE, SO THAT THEY MIGHT HEAR THE MOST HOLY OF PRONOUNCEMENTS. ⟩
"⟨ BUT, IT WAS NOT FATED TO BE THAT DAY. ⟩"
⟨ HOLY ONE! YOU MUST RUN! ESCAPE! ⟩
⟨ THE SCIENCE COUNCIL! THERE IS GREAT DANGER! ⟩

‹ PEACE NOW, SYRA. I'VE FACED THE COUNCIL'S WRATH BEFORE. ›
‹ BUT, THIS IS DIFFERENT, HOLY ONE. ›
‹ I BEG YOU, BEAR WITNESS TO MY MIND--SO THAT YOU CAN SEE. ›
‹ SO THAT YOU ALL CAN SEE! ›
"‹ I LEARNED OF THE PLOT WHILE PERFORMING MY DUTIES AS REGULATOR OF THE COUNCIL'S ROBOT DATA-BANKS! ›
"‹ THEY'VE DEVISED A STRANG NEW WEAPON, LIKE NOTHING HAVE EVER SEEN BEFORE. TH CALLED IT THE ERADICATOR. ›
"‹ THE DATA-BANKS VERIFIED THAT ITS POWER IS BEYOND THE MEASURE OF ALL KNOWN SCALES. ›
"‹ HOLY ONE, THEY MEAN TO KILL YOU WITH IT! ›"
‹ NO! THEY SHALL NOT KILL OUR TEACHER! ›
‹ WE WILL DESTROY THE COUNCIL! DEATH TO THEM ALL! ›
"‹ VIOLENCE WAS NEVER THE WAY OF THE DIVINE DEITY. I TRIED TO STILL THE RAGE WITHIN THEIR COLLECTIVE BREASTS, BUT, FOR ONCE, MY WORDS FAILED TO MOVE THEM. ›
"‹ AT LEAST, MOST OF THEM. ›"
‹ SEN-M, I WILL LEAD AN ASSAULT ON THE MAIN SCIENCE HALL. ARE YOU WITH US? ›
‹ DON'T YOU HEAR THE PRIEST'S WOR SYRA? WE'RE PLA ING RIGHT INTO TH COUNCIL'S HANDS
‹ THE COUNCIL HAS SHOWN THAT PEACEFUL WORDS HAVE NO WEIGHT WITH TO THEM. ›
‹ IF THIS PERSECUTION IS TO END, IT IS WE WHO MUST END IT--IN BLOOD! ›
"‹ SYRA'S WORDS BURNED LIKE A FEVER. ›
"‹ AS THE TEMPLE WALLS RUMBLED WITH THE ECHOES OF ANGER AND INDIGNATION, I STARED AT THE FADING IMAGE OF THE ERADICATOR... ›
"‹ ... SCIENCE AT ITS MOST OBSCENE. ›

RYPTONIAN SCIENCE AS JUST SHORT OF AGIC BY JOR-EL'S TIME.
HEN I THINK F HIM, IT'S S IF I CAN CTUALLY SEE HIM IN HIS ABORATORY..."
AMAZING!
AMAZING, MY LORD?
YES, KELEX-- THE HYPER-LIGHT DRIVE VEHICLE I HAVE DESIGNED...

...I DID NOT INTEND IT SO, BUT THIS CONFIGURATION IS REMARKABLY SIMILAR TO THAT OF A LEGENDARY MACHINE SUPPOSEDLY CONSTRUCTED DURING THE FIFTH HISTORIC EPOCH.
THE PURPOSES OF THE MACHINE-- IF IT TRULY DID EXIST-- ARE LOST TO ANTIQUITY. THAT MY WORK SHOULD SO RESEMBLE THAT OF THE ANCIENTS IS UNCANNY.

SURELY, SIRE, IT RESULTS FROM YOUR SUBCONSCIOUS RECALL OF THE ANCIENT DESIGN ELEMENTS.
PERHAPS, KELEX. THE SIMILARITIES ARE TOO GREAT TO BE COINCIDENTAL...

DON'T KNOW WHY I THOUGHT THAT... OR WHAT THAT EMORY WAS SUPPOSED TO GNIFY. I UNDERSTAND O LITTLE OF THE RYPTONIAN KNOWLEDGE HAT WAS GIVEN ME.
WORRY NOT ABOUT THE PAST--

--CONCENTRATE INSTEAD ON YOUR FUTURE. WHEN YOU RETURN TO THE FIELD, YOU WILL FACE DRAAGA!
HE IS MONGUL'S CHAMPION-- IF YOU DO NOT KILL HIM, YOU MUST DIE!
I MUST DIE, WHATEVER I DO...

...NONE OF US LIVE FOREVER.
?!?

⟨CLERIC, I HAVE AN IDEA!⟩
⟨THAT ALIEN GLADIATOR, SURELY IF YOU JUST ALLOW YOUR TWO MINDS TO CONNECT, TO SHARE EACH OTHER'S THOUGHTS... IT WILL PROVE...⟩
⟨CELLKEEPER, ALLOW ME TO FINISH MY TALE AND YOU WILL SEE WHY THAT LIFEFORM CANNOT POSSIBLY BE WHAT YOU THINK IT IS.⟩
⟨BESIDES, WHAT YOU ASK DEMANDS GREAT WILL-- AND I AM TOO OLD AND TIRED.⟩
⟨BUT, YOU HAVE TO TRY! TIME IS RUNNING OUT! MONGUL'S GAMES HAVE ALREADY STARTED!⟩
⟨PLEASE, CLERIC... WHAT IF YOU'RE WRONG?⟩
⟨DAMN YOUR INSOLENCE!⟩
⟨VERY WELL. I WILL PROVE IT TO YOU--ONCE AND FOR ALL!⟩
⟨BEAR WITNESS, CELL-KEEPER, AS THROUGH TH REACHES OF SPACE, MI MERGES WITH MIND.⟩
⟨WHAT IMAGES HIS MIND CONJURES I WILL SEE, AND IN TURN SO SHALL THE WINDOWS OF MY MIND BE OPEN TO HIM.⟩
⟨NOW!⟩
GREAT SCOTT!

HAT IS THE ATTER?

IMAGES... SENSATIONS... ARE BOMBARDING MY *MIND*! IS THIS SOME SORT OF CONDITIONING FOR THE GAMES?

I KNOW OF NO SUCH--!

WARRIORS TO THE FIELD! THE ***FINAL CONTEST*** COMMENCES!

‹CLERIC? ARE YOU ALL RIGHT?›

‹THE DIVINE DEITY FORGIVE ME-- WHAT HAVE I DONE?›

‹CLERIC!›

‹THE LINK... IS FORMED... THERE CAN BE NO... TURNING BACK...›

‹WE... ARE ...ONE...›

‹HEAR ME! IN THIS, THE FINAL CONTEST, MY CHAMPION SHALL EMERGE!›
‹DEVIATION FROM THE RULES WILL NOT BE TOLERATED! THE VICTOR MUST KILL HIS OPPONENT AND PRESENT HIS HEAD TO ME!›

‹LET THE GAME COMMENCE!›
TO THE DEATH!
TO THE DEATH!
TO THE DEATH

MY HEAD STILL ACHES FROM WHATEVER HIT ME -- I NEED A FEW SECONDS TO SHAKE IT OFF...
LOOK, PAL, I DON'T USE WEAPONS, AND I DON'T WANT THIS FIGHT!

DON'T YOU REALIZE HOW YOU'RE BEING USED? MONGUL HAS NO DIVINE HOLD OVER YOU! WE CAN LIBERATE THE OTHERS--
--DEPOSE THE TYRANT!

‹MONGUL IS CRUEL...›
‹HE COMMITS MANY ATROCITIES...›
JOIN WITH ME AGAINST HIM!

‹HE IS MY MASTER!›
‹I AM HIS CHAMPION!›

UNNGH! SHOULDN'T HAVE FALLEN FOR SUCH AN OBVIOUS PLOY... BUT MY HEAD... SO MIXED UP.
FEELS AS IF... SOMEONE'S FLIPPING THROUGH MY MEMORIES...
THE PROCEDURE CALLS FOR ONLY MOMENTARY EXPOSURE OF THE EPIDERMAL LAYER, JOR-EL. I CAN ASSURE YOU THERE WILL BE NO DISCOMFORT.

I AM NOT WORRIED, KELEX... BUT I AM EXCITED! HOW COULD I NOT BE?
TODAY, BY THE GRACE OF FATE AND THE WILL OF KRYPTON'S ELDERS, I AM TO FATHER A CHILD...

...PERHAPS THE HEALTHIEST CHILD KRYPTON HAS EVER KNOWN!

THERE IS NO QUESTION OF THAT! YOUR GENETIC PATTERN AND THAT OF THE LADY LARA WERE DETERMINED TO BE THE TWO STRONGEST ON KRYPTON!
THAT ATTERS LITTLE THE GREATER HEME OF THINGS, KELEX.
ALL THE BLOODLINES OF KRYPTON, I HAVE DISCOVERED, POSSESS A FLAW ...BUT IF MY CALCULATIONS ARE CORRECT--

--THE TREATMENTS I HAVE TAKEN WILL CORRECT THAT FLAW IN MY PROGENY.
AND MY CHILD WILL INHERIT THE COSMOS!

DESPERATELY, THE CHAMPION OF EARTH STRUGGLES TO CLEAR HIS HEAD, BUT THE IMAGES RACE ON...
FROM THE GATHERING OF JOR-EL'S CELL TISSUE BY ROBOTIC DOCTORS--

--TO ANOTHER TOWER, HUNDREDS OF MILES DISTANT...

...WHERE A SECOND MEDICAL TEAM SECURED GENETIC MATERIAL FROM THE WOMAN LARA.

CONGRATULATIONS, MY LADY. IT WILL BE A BOY.

THEIR PRECIOUS CARGO IN TOW, THE ROBOTS SPED ACROSS THE PLANET, TO KRYPTON'S REMOTE GESTATION CHAMBERS...

...THEIR EVERY MOVE MONITORED BY JOR-EL FROM AFAR VIA HOLOGRAPHIC VIEWER.

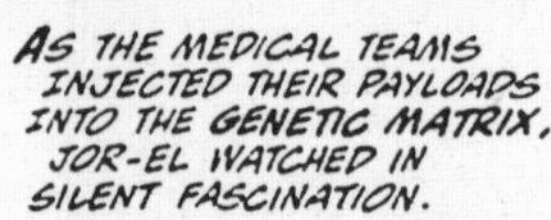
AS THE MEDICAL TEAMS INJECTED THEIR PAYLOADS INTO THE GENETIC MATRIX, JOR-EL WATCHED IN SILENT FASCINATION.

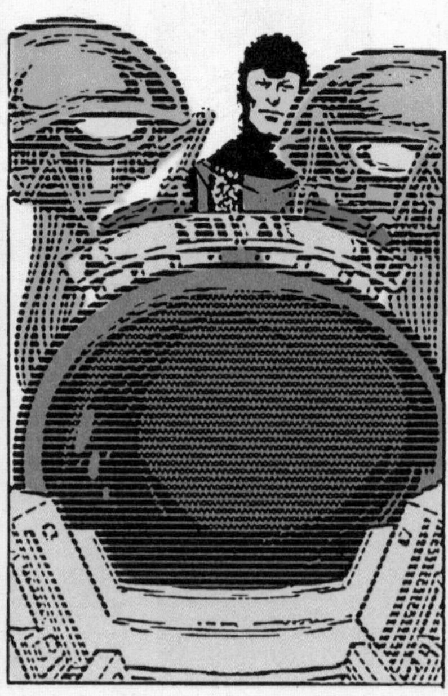

THROUGH THE MIND'S EYE OF KRYPTON'S LAST SON, THE OLD CLERIC WATCHES...

WHILE THE TAPESTRY OF A KRYPTON LOST TO HISTORY UNFURLS FROM THE MEMORY OF THE OLD CLERIC ...
... INTO THE MIND OF THE SON OF JOR-EL.
UNTIL HE, TOO, IS WITNESS TO THE DAY OF INTOLERANCE.

⟨STOP! IN THE NAME OF THE DIVINE DEITY, I BID YOU TO STOP!⟩
⟨THERE IS NO NEED FOR THIS! THE TIME OF DEPARTURE IS AT HAND!⟩
⟨HOLD YOUR FIRE! WHAT'S THAT FANATIC SAYING?⟩

⟨THE TIME HAS COME FOR ME TO RETURN TO MY SOLAR SYSTEM--BACK TO THE HOLY COMMUNE.⟩
⟨THE FAITHFUL WILL BE SAFE AND HAPPY THERE. AND KRYPTON WILL BE AS IT WAS.⟩
⟨LET NO BLOOD BE SPILLED IN MY NAME.⟩

⟨CLERIC, I DON'T KNOW WHY, BUT I BELIEVE YOU.⟩
⟨PERHAPS IT IS...⟩
⟨NO!⟩

⟨SCIENCE AND SUPERSTITION CANNOT CO-EXIST! IT IS NOT LOGICAL!⟩

‹FOR THE COUNCIL TO SURVIVE...›
‹RELIGIOUS FANATICISM MUST BE ERADICATED!›
"‹I WAS CARELESS. MY BODY CONVULSED WITH THE SPASMS OF INTENSE, ALL-CONSUMING PAIN.›
"‹YET, MIRACULOUS I DID NOT DIE.
"‹BUT OTHERS DID. SO MANY DID.›
"‹FOR INTOLERANCE-- BE IT OF SCIENCE OR FAITH-- KILLS!›
"‹WHAT HAPPENED NEXT IS STILL A PUZZLE TO ME.›"
‹HALT! YOU ARE DOING THAT WRONG! DON'T UNDO THE POSITIONING THAT WAY!›
‹YOU'RE CORRUPTING THE ERADICATOR MATRIX!›
‹IT'S GOING TO...›
NOOOOO!

DRAAGA! DRAAGA!
‹THE KRYPTON-MAN IS DISTRACTED, TIRED!›
‹DRAAGA IS A GREAT CHAMPION!›
‹TOO GOOD, IT SEEMS...›

...I TIRE OF HIM -- IT WOULD BE XCITING TO SEE HIM DEFEATED!"›

‹YOUR REFUSAL TO KILL IS YOUR WEAKNESS!›

‹YOUR RACE DESERVES EXTINCTION!›

‹A RACE OF COWARDS WHO DO NOT MERIT A WARRIOR'S DEATH!›

⟨YES! STAND AND FACE ME...⟩
⟨...THIS ENDS NOW!⟩
IT'S JUST STARTED, DRAAGA!
⟨YAAARGH!⟩
NO WEAPO HAND HAND C BAT
AND WHERE DO YOU GET OFF CALLING ME A COWARD...
...WHEN YOU'RE THE ONE WHO'S AFRAID TO STAND UP TO MONGUL?
⟨"THIS HAS TURNED OUT TO BE A WORTHY MATCH AFTER ALL. THE CHALLENGER HAS BEEN FEIGNING WEAKNESS UNTIL NOW!"⟩

⟨HE'S AFTER BLOOD!⟩
⟨HE'LL KILL!⟩
⟨TEN UNITS SAYS HE WON'T!⟩
⟨DRAAGA IS NOT DEFEATED YET! HE'LL RALLY!⟩

⟨"LOOK AT GREAT MONGUL ON HIS THRONE, SMILING, CONFIDENT IN HIS CHAMPION."⟩
THE SLAVE HAS THE FIRE AFTER ALL-- DRAAGA MERELY NEEDED TO PROVOKE...⟩

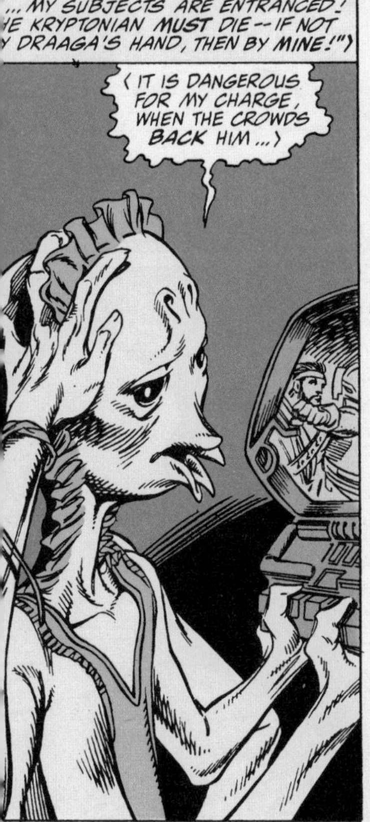
...MY SUBJECTS ARE ENTRANCED! HE KRYPTONIAN MUST DIE--IF NOT Y DRAAGA'S HAND, THEN BY MINE!"⟩
⟨IT IS DANGEROUS FOR MY CHARGE, WHEN THE CROWDS BACK HIM...⟩

⟨THEY SEAL HIS FATE! MONGUL WILL NOT BE CHALLENGED BY HIS POPULARITY!⟩

MY HEAD! NOT AGAIN--
--IMAGES FLOODING IN--A SMOKING RUINS...

"⟨AS THE VIBRATIONS OF THE AWESOME BLAST BEGAN TO SPUTTER AND DIE, I COULD HEAR THE MOURNFUL WAIL OF A KRYPTONIAN HOVERCRAFT.⟩
"⟨IT FLITTED ABOUT LIKE A SKITTISH BIRD, SEARCHING FOR SOME LEVEL GROUND ON WHICH TO REST.⟩
"⟨AFTER SEVERAL ATTEMPTS, THE SHIP LANDED AND DEGORGED ITSELF OF ITS CREW.⟩
"⟨THEN, I HEARD THE PAINED VOICE OF NOBLE SEN-M.⟩"
⟨SYRA! SYRA! WHERE ARE YOU?!⟩
⟨BY THE DIVINE DEITY.⟩
⟨NO!⟩
⟨SYRA!!⟩
⟨...SYRA...⟩

THE TIME FOR MOURNING MUST BE BRIEF, MY FAITHFUL CHILDREN:).
FOR THE COUNCIL WILL SURELY BLAME US FOR THIS SLAUGHTER -- AND SEEK VENGEANCE.)
(CLERIC!)
(YES, THE DIVINE DEITY HAS SEEN FIT TO SPARE MY UNWORTHY LIFE.)
(SO THAT I MAY LEAD YOU FROM KRYPTON'S DARKNESS -- TO THE LIGHT OF THE HOLY COMMUNE.)
(AND WE SHALL TAKE THIS WITH US. UNTIL KRYPTON HAS MATURED, IT CANNOT BE TRUSTED WITH SUCH A DEADLY TOY.)
(THE GREAT ARK AWAITS. ARE YOU WITH ME?)
WE SHALL FOLLOW YOU TO ETERNITY, HOLY ONE. WE ARE READY.)
(DEAR CLERIC, I MUST, MOST RESPECTFULLY, DECLINE.)
(KRYPTON IS A WORLD ON THE BRINK. SURELY SOMEONE SHOULD REMAIN... TO SPREAD THE FAITH... TO CHALLENGE THE CLONERS.)
(PLEASE, HOLY ONE. I CANNOT LET OUR WORDS DIE HERE.)
"(SO, SEN-M AND HIS FELLOW APOSTLES REMAINED ON KRYPTON. I SORROWED AT LEAVING SUCH A GALLANT, LOYAL SOUL BEHIND, BUT I COULD NOT FORCE HIM TO GO AGAINST HIS OWN HEART.)
"(WITH OVER A HUNDRED-THOUSAND KRYPTONIANS IN ITS BELLY, THE GREAT ARK CLIMBED INTO THE WAITING HEAVENS...)
"(...BOUND FOR PARADISE...)
"(...BUT DAMNED TO HELL.)"

"THE SHIP--SO HUGE. WHY DON'T I REMEMBER?
"MY FATHER TOLD OF KRYPTON'S HISTORY, BUT THIS IMAGE IS NOT HIS!"

‹YOUR BLOOD MARKS MY FIST, KRYPTONIAN!›

‹THE LAST BLOOD OF YOUR LINE, YET YOU HAVE NO FIGHT LEFT FOR ME?›
"THESE ARE NOT MY MEMORIES!"

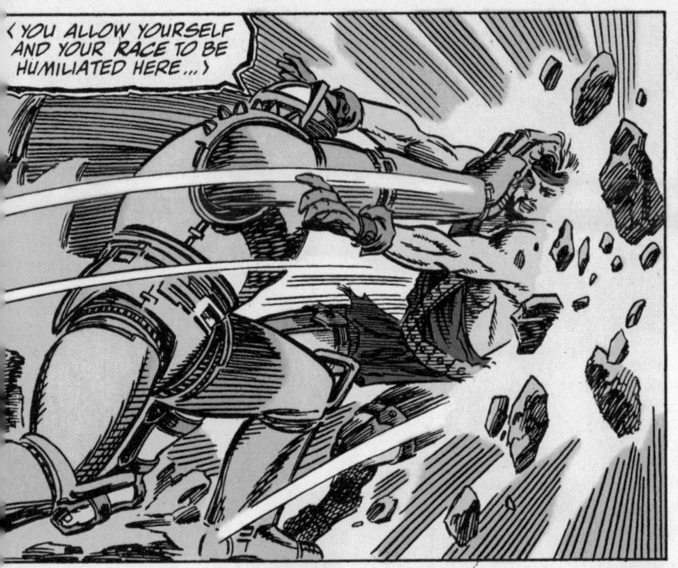
‹YOU ALLOW YOURSELF AND YOUR RACE TO BE HUMILIATED HERE...›

"THESE IMAGES ARE HIS, THE INTRUDER'S --NOT MY FATHER'S!

MEMORIES OF THINGS ATHER NEVER TOLD ME..."

‹ALREADY THE CROWD CALLS FOR YOUR END!›

"WHY? WHY DID YOU NEVER TELL ME THESE THINGS, FATHER?"
‹DRAAGA NOWS HOW TO PLAY OUT THE OMENT--MAKE YOU WANT DEATH AS BADLY AS THEY DO!›

WHY?
MY SON ... THE WAR AND BLOODSHED WHICH SWEPT KRYPTON DURING ITS SIXTH HISTORIC EPOCH GREW FROM THE ANCIENTS' CONCERN OVER A GREAT MORAL QUESTION.

A THOUSAND CENTURIES BEFORE YOUR CONCEPTION, THE BLACK ZERO TERRORISTS INITIATED THE WARS, FLASHING SLOGANS BORN A THOUSAND CENTURIES BEFORE THEM--
FULL MIND FULL LIFE
NO SPARE PARTS

--IN THE WRITINGS OF SEN-M, A FAMOUS TEACHER OF THE FIFTH EPOCH. A PACIFIST, SEN-M WOULD HAVE BEEN HORRIFIED BY THE CRIMES COMMITTED IN HIS NAME.

INTERESTINGLY, THERE EXIST FRAGMENTS OF REPORTS THAT SEN-M WAS HIMSELF THE FOLLOWER OF A HOLY MAN FROM ANOTHER WORLD...
... BUT THIS IS THE STUFF OF LEGEND.

‹SO. THAT IS THE SOLE SUM OF MY MISSION TO KRYPTON.›
‹A MERE UESTION MARK N THE DATABANKS OF HISTORY... FORGOTTEN... DISAVOWED...›
‹A FITTING PUNISHMENT, I SUPPOSE...›
‹AFTER WHAT HAPPENED ON THE ARK, IT WOULD HAVE SERVED THE DIVINE DEITY BETTER IF I HAD NEVER EXISTED.›

"‹IT ALL SEEMED SO ROUTINE. THE GREAT ARK BROKE FROM THE PULL OF THE HOME PLANET'S GRAVITY, AS IT HAD DONE ON SO MANY OTHER MISSIONS.›
"‹CHORUSES OF JUBILANT CELEBRATION ECHOED THROUGHOUT THE SHIP.›"

HOLY ONE, WE RE SO EXCITED! OW LONG WILL THIS JOURNEY BE?›
‹MY WIFE AND I LOOK FORWARD TO RAISING OUR CHILD ON THE HOLY SOIL!›
"‹IT WAS SO WONDERFUL.›

"‹BUT THEN, IT ALL ENDED...›"
‹CLERIC... I-I FEEL... STRANGE...›
‹TYR-N! WHAT'S WRONG?!›
‹PAIN ...OH... SUCH... PAIN...›

"‹...HORRIBLY... SUDDENLY...›"
‹TYR-N!›

"⟨ WITHIN MOMENTS, VOICES WHICH HAD CAROLED OUT SONGS OF ELATION SHRIEKED WITH CRIES OF TERROR AND ANGUISH. ⟩

"⟨ THEY WERE **DYING**. ALL OF THEM. A HUNDRED THOUSAND MEN, WOMEN AND CHILDREN. EVERY LAST ONE OF THEM. ⟩

"⟨ I WIELDED ALL MY MYSTIC POWER, POWER ENDOWED ME BY THE HOLY TRIBUNAL ITSELF... ⟩

"⟨ ... BUT IT WAS USELESS. ⟩

"⟨ AGAIN AND AGAIN-- ⟩ôïïøπıooıū=ΔΔ⟨-- RANG OUT... THE ANCIENT KRYPTONIAN **DEATH CHANT**. ⟩

"KAL-EL, MY SON, THERE IS A DEFECT IN THE KRYPTONIAN GENOTYPE WHICH HAS TIED US TO THIS PLANET. TO LEAVE OUR WORLD'S ENVIRONS HAS MEANT DEATH.
"TREATMENTS THAT I TOOK PRIOR TO YOUR CONCEPTION HAVE ELIMINATED THAT DEFECT IN YOU. I HAD HOPES THAT YOU WOULD TAKE KRYPTON TO THE STARS, BUT NOW...
"THERE IS MUCH I WOULD SAY TO YOU, AND SO LITTLE TIME.

"OUR ANCESTORS THOUGHT THEY HAD ENDED THE MENACE OF BLACK ZERO EONS AGO. BUT BEFORE ITS DEMISE, THAT CULT HAD TRIGGERED A NUCLEAR DEVICE--

"-- WHICH, I BELIEVE, STARTED A CHAIN REACTION DEEP WITHIN OUR PLANET'S CORE, CREATING A NEW AND DEADLY RADIOACTIVE ELEMENT.

"TWENTY MILLION KRYPTONIANS HAVE DIED WITHIN THE PAST CYCLE.

"KRYPTON IS KILLING US.

TODAY, MY FEARS WERE CONFIRMED.
"KRYPTON ITSELF WILL SOON DIE.

"ONLY YOU CAN ESCAPE OUR DOOM. THESE PAST MONTHS, MY ROBOTS HAVE CONSTRUCTED THE STAR DRIVE I DESIGNED YEARS AGO.

"YOUR MOTHER HAS JOINED ME... SHE KNOWS WHAT I HAVE DONE, AND--IN HER OWN WAY-- I THINK SHE UNDERSTANDS.
"I HAVE BEAMED THIS RECORDING OF MY THOUGHTS AND DREAMS INTO THE VEHICLE WHICH WILL CARRY YOUR BIRTHING MATRIX TO A NEW WORLD, THAT YOU MAY ONE DAY LEARN OF US.

"YOUR MOTHER AND I SHALL FACE DEATH TOGETHER IN PRAYER..."

"REMEMBER US.
"FAREWELL."

(STAND AND ACCEPT DEATH, KRYPTONIAN!)
DEATH?
TOO MUCH DEATH-- MY MOTHER, MY FATHER.
MY WHOLE PLANET DIED!
I'M THE SOLE HEIR OF KRYPTON...
...HER LAST SON!
I AM KAL-EL!

"WHILE KRYPTON WENT TO ITS DOOM, I ALONE SURVIVED--

"--SENT ACROSS SPACE TO EARTH...

"...THERE TO BE BORN AND RAISED A MAN!"

‹I HAD DISGRACED MY FAITH. I COULDN'T GO BACK TO THE COMMUNE.›
‹SO I CAME HERE, AND BECAME AS THE ROCK-- COLD AND LIFELESS. AND EONS OLD.›

‹AND DURING ALL THOSE EONS, THE ERADICATOR HAS REMAINED WITH ME. I NEVER REALLY KNEW WHY I'D KEPT IT FOR SO LONG.›

‹BUT NOW, IT IS ALL CLEAR.›

MY NAME, TYRANT, IS SUPERMAN--
AND I DON'T KILL!

THE ERADICATOR
ND THE MATRIX-
RAFT--THE RESEM-
LANCE IS NOT A
OINCIDENCE. AND
HE KRYPTONIAN
DEATH CRY...⟩
⟨IT'S TRUE! AFTER ALL THESE CEN-TURIES, MY PRAYERS HAVE FINALLY BEEN ANSWERED!⟩
⟨HEAR ME, LAST SON OF KRYPTON! AND BEAR WITNESS TO ...YOUR DESTINY!⟩
⟨YOUR REFUSAL LEAVES ME NO RECOURSE BUT TO KILL YOU BOTH MYSELF!⟩
I'M NOT AFRAID OF YOU, MONGUL! COME DOWN FROM THAT THRONE OF YOURS AND FACE ME ONE ON ONE!
TO BE CONTINUED IN THE PAGES OF SUPERMAN #32!
ON SALE NEXT WEEK!

DC
SUPERMAN
THE MAN OF STEEL
100
MAY 00
APPROVED BY THE COMICS CODE AUTHORITY
2000
20
THE NEW FORTRESS OF SOLITUDE REVEALED!
DM '00
tom
SCHULTZ
MAHNKE
NGUYEN

THE BEGINNING IS A FRIGHTENING TIME.
KOFF, KOFF

I--UM-- I NEED TO BE GONE FOR AWHILE, LOIS...
...BUSINESS...
KOFF

WHATEVER. DON'T LET THE DOOR HIT YOUR CAPE ON THE WAY OUT.
AND CAN'T YOU HAVE KELEX CHECK OUT THAT WRETCHED COUGH?
...WATCH ME PULL A RABBIT OUTTA...

...MY HAT. NOTHIN' UP MY SLEEVE...
UH, OH. LOOK AT THE TIME, NATASHA. DUTY CALLS...
HEH, HEH...

GUY, UNC! THE NEXT EPISODE IS A CLASSIC!
I KNOW, I KNOW--BUT TIME WAITS FOR NO SUPERMAN.
NOW YOU REMEMBER THE DRILL. WE'LL BE BACK BY MORNING AND I NEED YOU TO HAVE THE STEELWORKS UP AND RUNNING...

THE BEGINNING IS ALWAYS A FRIGHTENING TIME. IN THE CRUCIBLE OF CREATION, CHAOS RULES--THE UNKNOWN AND THE TERRIBLE HAUNT AND PREY UPON A DISORIENTED MANKIND. FORCES THAT CAN NOT BE BE CONTROLLED STALK THE LAND.
...SO WHEN THE CTESSON PARTICLES GENERATED BY OUR HEMICLOUD CHAMBER EXCITE THE PROBABILITY FIELD ASSOCIATED WITH THE TRACE SINGULARITY...
...THE RESULTING POLARITY REVERSAL SHOULD SLIDE THE GHOST DOWN INTO OUR PLASMA TRAP.
UNDERSTAND?
IN THE BEGINNING, A VULNERABLE MANKIND MUST LOOK TO ITS HEROES. THE NAVAJO TURNED TO THEIR TWIN WAR-GODS TO PROTECT THEIR BELEAGUERED HOME FROM MONSTERS AND ALIEN GODS.
NO.
THAT'S WHY I ASKED FOR YOUR HELP.
BUT IT'S VERY SIMPLE IF YOU JUST VISUALIZE THE QUANTUM GRID IN TERMS OF A 4-DIMENSIONAL NEO-PLANCK EQUATION...
...THE PROTO-GREEKS SURVIVED THANKS TO THE BROTHER TITANS PROMETHEUS AND EPIMETHEUS, WHO DELIVERED POWER, AND FIRE, AND HOPE TO MANKIND...
STEEL--I DON'T KNOW THAT I'M EVER GOING TO COMPREHEND THE WHY BEHIND ALL OF THIS...
I'M JUST GLAD IT STILL EXISTS--AND CAN BE RETRIEVED.
OH, WE CAN DO MORE THAN JUST RETRIEVE IT...
...AND THE ANCIENT KRYPTONIAN BOLMETH PEOPLE CREDIT THEIR GOLDEN AGE TO A BENEVOLENT COLLABORATION BETWEEN YLA-UTH, THE SUN-LORD AND KOR-OP, THE EARTH-GIANT.
...ONCE THE TRACE SINGULARITY HAS BEEN CAPTURED IN THE SPECTRAL NEXUS APPARATUS' STABILIZATIC CHAMBER...
DIFFERENT TIMES, DIFFERENT WORLDS, DIFFERENT CULTURES-- BUT THE STORY ALWAYS REMAINS THE SAME. THE BEGINNING IS A DELICATE THING, AND SO MUCH CAN GO WRONG...

Creation Story
MARK SCHULTZ writer
DOUG MAHNKE penciller
TOM NGUYEN inker
KEN LOPEZ letterer
GLENN WHITMORE WILDSTORM FX colors
MAUREEN McTIGUE associate editor
EDDIE BERGANZA editor
Special Thanks to LOUISE SIMONSON & JON BOGDANOVE for getting us here & JOEL MOEN, PAT GLEASON, GORDON PURCELL and SHAWN MOLL!
...ONCE THE GHOST IS IN THE BOTTLE...
...WE'RE CARTING IT BACK TO METROPOLIS AND BUILDING YOU THE BEST FORTRESS OF SOLITUDE A SUPERMAN EVER HAD!
SUPERMAN created by JERRY SIEGEL and JOE SHUSTER

KELEX CALLED IT A **GHOST FORTRESS** BECAUSE HE SAID IT WAS LIKE THE SOUL OF A MAN WHO COULDN'T ACCEPT HIS OWN DEATH, JOHN.
NOT A BAD ANALOGY. THE INCREDIBLE POWER RELEASED WITH THE STRIKE OF LUTHOR'S KRYPTONITE MISSILE--
--SHOCKED THE ANNIHILATED **MATERIAL BODY** OF THE FORTRESS INTO PERMANENTLY HOLDING TO WHAT **SHOULD** HAVE BEEN A TRANSITORY STATE ON ITS WAY TO PURE, RELEASED ENERGY...
...AND THUS, ALLOWING US TO NOW COLLECT THE **ATOMIC MEMORY** OF EVERYTHING THAT EVER EXISTED IN THE FORTRESS.
KOFF
WISH **YOU'D** HAVE KELEX CHECK THAT COUGH.
I'M ALL RIGHT.
KOFF
IN THE **BEGINNING**, THE NEW WORLD GROWS FROM THE ASHES OF THE OLD. BUT EVEN AS **LAW**, **LOGIC** AND **ORDER** TAKE FORM, THE AGENTS OF **ANARCHY**, OF UNBRIDLED CREATION, REMAIN UNDETERRED.
...THEY ARE CALLED **TRICKSTER--COYOTE--UTGARD-LOKI...**
010111101001 011110001010 101001010100 10100...

...THEY ARE THE FOOT SOLDIERS OF CHAOS.
...0101111010010 1111000101010100 101010010100...
OUR WEEKS OF OF INFILTRATION AND METICULOUS OBSERVATION WILL FINALLY PAY OFF, LUNA...
OF COURSE. THERE WAS NEVER A DOUBT.
EXCELLENT.
VERY GOOD. POLYPHEMUS 212 REPORTS THAT THE CAPTURE WAS SUCCESSFUL.
IN ADDITION TO THE BRAINIAC 13 TECHNOLOGY WE CONTINUE TO UNLOCK, WE'LL SOON POSSESS THE SECRETS OF KRYPTONIAN SCIENCE.
WE MOVE CLOSER, CYBERMOTHS! CLOSER TO THE DAY WHEN WE SEIZE METROPOLIS!
ALL HAIL LUNA, QUEEN OF THE CYBERNETIC UNDERGROUND!
ALL HAIL ME, YOU BET.
IS IT READY, SPHINX 44? AM I SET TO SPEAK WITH HE WHO CALLS THE SHOTS?
THE OVERMIND IS WAITING, LUNA...

"...CRYPTO-MODEM ENGAGED!"
HE WHO CALLS THE SHOTS??
A POOR ATTEMPT AT HUMOR, OBSCURE ONE.
THE TENSION HERE IS THICK ENOUGH TO CUT.

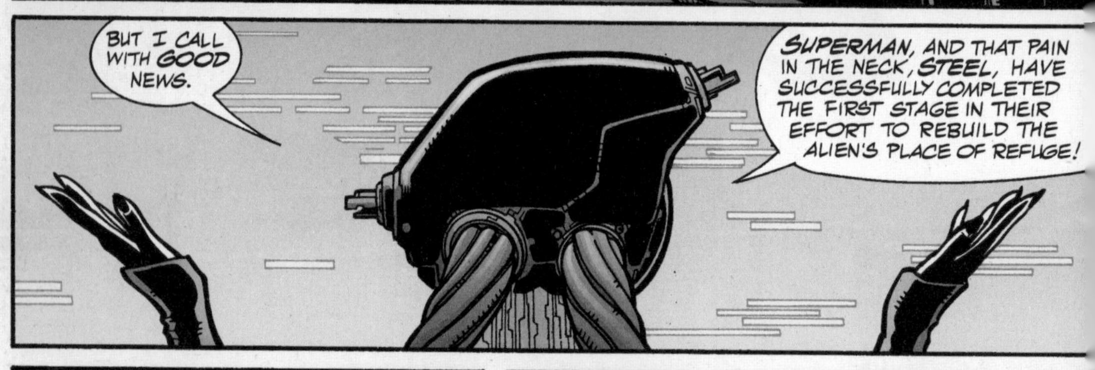
BUT I CALL WITH GOOD NEWS.
SUPERMAN, AND THAT PAIN IN THE NECK, STEEL, HAVE SUCCESSFULLY COMPLETED THE FIRST STAGE IN THEIR EFFORT TO REBUILD THE ALIEN'S PLACE OF REFUGE!

I SEE.
AND YOU WERE PLANNING TO BRING ME UP TO DATE ON THE COURSE OF OUR OPERATION IN THAT ARENA? OR MUST I...
UNCLENCH YOUR OVERBROW, MY OVERMIND. APOLOGIES FOR MY NEGLIGENCE.
ALLOW ME TO BRING YOU UP TO SPEED...

...TWO WEEKS AGO, AGENT GYPSY 84 MANAGED TO GAIN ACCESS TO THE ANNOYING STEEL'S LABORATORIES--
--WHERE, INCREDIBLY ENOUGH, HE WITNESSED OUR ANTAGONIST MIDWIFING THE BIRTH OF A TESSERACT--

"CONTINUING TO OVERRIDE THE STEELWORKS' 813 TRANSMODED SECURITY SYSTEMS, GYPSY 84 LEARNED OF SUPERMAN AND STEEL'S PLANS FOR THIS POCKET DIMENSION...
...INFINITE SPACE WITHIN A FINITE DIMENSIONAL CONTAINMENT! I'VE SEEN THEM IN THE FUTURE.
IF MY FORTRESS COULD BE REBUILT WITHIN THERE-- WOULD THAT BE POSSIBLE?
WELL, THEORETICALLY YES -- BUT...
"...THEY STRUCK A DEAL-- FORMED A PARTNERSHIP...
THIS IS KELEX. HE HOLDS THE FORTRESS' COMPLETE COMPUTER FILES IN HIS MEMORY.
MY KNOWLEDGE OF KRYPTONIAN SCIENCE COUPLED WITH YOUR ENGINEERING SKILLS CAN MAKE THIS HAPPEN, MASTER IRONS.
WHILE WHO PAYS THE BILLS?
"...AND BEGAN ACTUALIZING THE CONTROLLED REBIRTH OF KRYPTONIAN TECHNOLOGY ON EARTH.
IT'S A SOLITON-GENERATOR-- IT ALLOWED ME TO ESCAPE THE PHANTOM ZONE.
I SUPPOSE ITS FUNCTION COULD BE RECONFIGURED INTO THAT OF AN INTER-DIMENSIONAL PORTAL.
EXCUSE ME, MISTRESS NATASHA, BUT THE MASTERS WILL BE NEEDING ME...
THE MASTERS, HUH? SOMEONE NEEDS THEIR SOCIAL AWARENESS RESPONSE RECALIBRATED.

"WHILE STEEL AND THE ROBOT BRAINSTORMED THE SCIENCE OF RECONSTRUCTION, SUPERMAN WOULD DISAPPEAR REPEATEDLY TO WHO KNOWS WHERE...
TO REMATERIALIZE THE FORTRESS, JOHN HENRY SAYS WE'LL NEED TONS OF RAW MATERIALS...
...THE COPPER LEFT IN THIS ABANDONED MINE WILL BE A START.
KRUMPF
KRUNCH
"...RETURNING WITH HUGE QUANTITIES OF THE STUFF FROM WHICH THE GHOST FORTRESS WILL DRAW MOLECULAR SUBSTANCE.
NATASHA! WHAT ARE YOU...?
OH, JUST MAKING A MINOR RESPONSE ALTERATION.
IT'LL MAKE FOR A MORE WELL-ADJUSTED SUPPORT TEAM-- RIGHT, KELEX?
SPRRRK
"THEY HAVE WORKED NONSTOP ON THIS PROJECT, CHALLENGING OUR ABILITY TO KEEP PACE."
THE QUANTUM RADICAL GOVERNOR WILL NEED ADJUSTMENTS, KELEX.
WILL DO.
THE GIFFLER WRENCH, BIG BLUE. SHAKE A LEG.

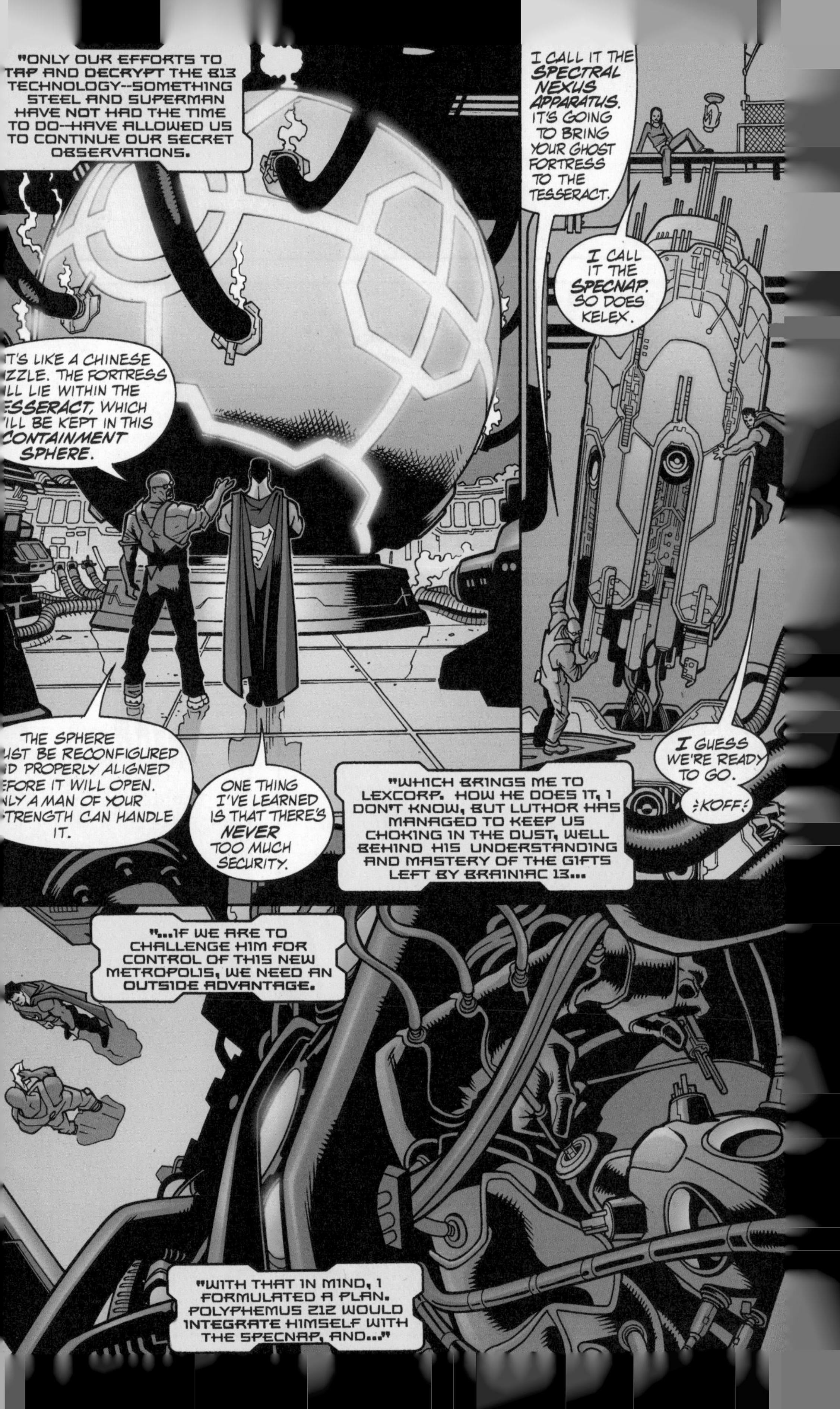
"ONLY OUR EFFORTS TO TAP AND DECRYPT THE B13 TECHNOLOGY--SOMETHING STEEL AND SUPERMAN HAVE NOT HAD THE TIME TO DO--HAVE ALLOWED US TO CONTINUE OUR SECRET OBSERVATIONS.
I CALL IT THE SPECTRAL NEXUS APPARATUS. IT'S GOING TO BRING YOUR GHOST FORTRESS TO THE TESSERACT.
I CALL IT THE SPECNAP. SO DOES KELEX.
T'S LIKE A CHINESE ZZLE. THE FORTRESS LL LIE WITHIN THE ESSERACT, WHICH ILL BE KEPT IN THIS CONTAINMENT SPHERE.
THE SPHERE UST BE RECONFIGURED D PROPERLY ALIGNED EFORE IT WILL OPEN. NLY A MAN OF YOUR TRENGTH CAN HANDLE IT.
ONE THING I'VE LEARNED IS THAT THERE'S NEVER TOO MUCH SECURITY.
"WHICH BRINGS ME TO LEXCORP. HOW HE DOES IT, I DON'T KNOW, BUT LUTHOR HAS MANAGED TO KEEP US CHOKING IN THE DUST, WELL BEHIND HIS UNDERSTANDING AND MASTERY OF THE GIFTS LEFT BY BRAINIAC 13...
I GUESS WE'RE READY TO GO.
KOFF
"...IF WE ARE TO CHALLENGE HIM FOR CONTROL OF THIS NEW METROPOLIS, WE NEED AN OUTSIDE ADVANTAGE.
"WITH THAT IN MIND, I FORMULATED A PLAN. POLYPHEMUS 212 WOULD INTEGRATE HIMSELF WITH THE SPECNAP, AND..."

I HAVE BEEN IN CONTACT WITH A DISTANT-OTHER.
ENOUGH. WE'VE ALREADY DISCUSSED YOUR PLAN.
HE IS EAGER TO BE FREE TO AVENGE HIMSELF ON SUPERMAN, BUT BE AWARE...

...HIS WINDOW OF OPPORTUNITY IS VERY NARROW, AND SO YOUR TIMING MUST BE PRECISE.
NOW GO! BRING ME THIS TECHNOLOGY THAT WILL DELIVER METROPOLIS FROM LUTHOR'S HANDS...

...AND INTO OURS!
SO BE IT, YOUR OVERMINDEDNESS! IT'S SHOW TIME!
CYBERMOTHS! WHAT IS TRUE POWER?

KNOWLEDGE IS TRUE POWER!!
THEY THAT CONTROL THE INFORMATION STREAM HOLD THE HIGH GROUND!!

BEWARE THE TRICKSTER--HE IS A SHAPE-SHIFTER.
SO I STILL DON'T UNDERSTAND WHY YOU DIDN'T JUST GO TO THE JLA WITH THE PROJECT...
JOHN HENRY, THE JLA IS FINE IN ITS PLACE--BUT IT--CAN BE *KOFF* --
--I NEED SOMEONE CLOSE WHO CAN MONITOR METROPOLIS WHEN I'M CALLED AWAY.

YOU'RE GOOD AT WHAT YOU DO.
I KNOW I CAN TRUST YOU TO BE DISCREET WITH KRYPTONIAN SECRETS, AND I THOUGHT THE STEELWORKS COULD BECOME A SORT OF LOCAL SUBSTATION OF THE FORTRESS...
WELL, FAR BE IT FROM ME TO SAY NO TO AN INFUSION OF KRYPTONIAN SCIENCE. SHOULD HELP GET THE B13 BUGS UNDER CONTROL.

...INITIATE TOTAL INTEGRATION PROCESS, POLYPHEMUS 212--REPEAT...

ON EARTH HE IS REGARDED AS A MAGICAL BEING...
...INITIATE TOTAL INTEGRATION...
...PREPARE TO SEIZE COMMAND AND RELEASE THE OTHER...

...BUT ON KRYPTON HE WAS ASSOCIATED WITH THE TERRIFYING ENERGIES OF THE ELECTROMAGNETIC FIELD ITSELF.
...DO NOT DISAPPOINT YOUR COMRADES, POLYPHEMUS 212...

BY SHIFTING TO IMITATE THE FAMILIAR, BY MELDING WITH THE TRUSTED, THE TRICKSTER GUARANTEES HIS WELCOME TO HEARTH AND HOME.
HEADS UP, NAT! WE'RE BACK!
HOW WAS YOUR "CLASSIC EPISODE"?
EVEN FUNNIER THAN THE LAST TIME I SAW IT.
BUT NOT AS DEEPLY MEANINGFUL WITHOUT YOU THERE.
WE'RE READY TO RUMBLE, OH, AUTHORITY FIGURES...
...ALL FIRED UP AND THE POT'S ON THE STOVE.
PLEASE MOVE YOUR BUTT, BIG BLUE.
THEN LET'S GET THIS SHOW ON THE ROAD!
OPEN THE CONTAINMENT SPHERE--ACCESS THE TESSERACT!

URRY! THE OONER WE ET THE HOST ORTRESS ROJECTED, E BETTER.
IKE WE RACTICED-- OTH OF OU WILL GO NSIDE.
THE REVERSED SPECNAP WILL DISGORGE THE GHOST FORTRESS INTO THE TESSERACT...
...AND CARRY YOU ALONG WITH IT.
ONCE INSIDE, IT'S UP TO YOU TO ACTIVATE OUR CONSTRUCTION PROGRAM!
NATASHA-- LET 'ER RIP!
IT WORKED, KELEX!
WE'RE BACK IN THE GHOST FORTRESS!
FRESH.

THEY'RE IN!
BUT-- THIS IS STRANGE--
--I'M GETTING SOME EXOTIC READINGS...

TASHA-- DO A VISUAL INSPECTION OF THE SPECNAP...
A VISUAL INSPECTION? CHEEEEEZ!
TASH...

OKAY, OKAY.
LIKE I'M REALLY GOING TO FIND ANYTHING...
...LIKE, WHILE YOU WERE FLYING IT HERE, YOU MIGHT HAVE DROPPED IT OR SOMETHING...
LIKE I'M...
...EWWW...
UNC...?
THAT-- IS NOT GOOD...
...GOT TO ALERT SUPER...
I THINK NOT, DR. IRONS...

I THINK EVERYTHING IS JUST FINE AS IS.
AND SO THE TRICKSTER PREPARES THE WAY FOR THE ADVENT OF CHAOS.
THE MOTHS?!
THE CYBERMOTHS.
AND I AM LUNA, YOUR OFFICIAL CYBERMOTH REPRESENTATIVE.
YOU'VE BEEN QUITE THE THORN IN OUR SIDE, DR. IRONS, WHAT WITH YOUR HABITUAL DISRUPTIONS OF OUR DIGITAL SIPHONING OPERATIONS...
...BUT NOW I THINK YOUR SCIENTIFIC PROWESS WILL DO US SOME GOOD.
PLEASE DON'T GO TRYING ANYTHING HEROIC--YOU MAY BE BULLETPROOF IN THAT ARMOR, BUT I DOUBT YOUR NIECE IS.

HOW...? WHY...?

HOW? THROUGH A SUPERIOR KNOWLEDGE OF THE INFRASTRUCTURE CHANGES WROUGHT BY THE B13 VIRUS.
WE KNOW YOUR SYSTEMS BETTER THAN YOU DO.
WE OWN YOUR SECURITY PROGRAMS.

WHY? BECAUSE WE CAN.

THAT'S ALL YOU NEED TO KNOW FOR NOW, SCIENCE BOY.
CHAINS, PLEASE...

STAY COOL, JOHN HENRY-- BIDE YOUR TIME...
CONTACT POLYPHEMUS 212 AND TELL HIM THE STEELWORKS HAS BEEN SECURED.
WE ARE READY AND WILLING TO JUMP AS SOON AS HE'S OPENED THE PORTAL.

HERE THEY COME, KELEX-- RIGHT ON SCHEDULE...
...THE "GHOSTS" OF ROBOT SECURITY...
...ATTACKING LIKE ANTIBODIES ON A MICROBE.
BRRRR! CONTACT DOESN'T FEEL ANY BETTER NOW THAN IT DID ON OUR FIRST TRIP INTO THIS NETHERWORLD.
I'D APPRECIATE IT IF YOU'D COMPLETE YOUR PARTICLE LINK A.S.A.P.
IN MAN OF STEEL #90-- ED
CHILL, BLUE.
INTERSTITIAL COMPUTER LINKAGE IS COMING ON LINE.
THE FORTRESS COMPUTERS NOW RECOGNIZE AND ACCEPT US...
...AND I HAVE ENGAGED THE CONSTRUCTION PROGRAM DESIGNED BY UNCLE JOHN AND MY OWN BAD SELF.
OBSERVE--HERE COME THE TONS AND TONS OF RAW MATTER NEEDED TO BUILD THE BONES OF A HEALTHY, GROWING FORTRESS.
KICK IT!

THE IRON ORE RESERVES HAVE STARTED TO MOVE!
IT'S BEGUN THEN.
SUPERMAN IS GETTING HIS VACATION HOME BACK!
AMAZING...
...JUST AMAZING...
IT ALL SEEMS TO BE HAPPENING ALMOST TOO FAST...
...AND THE SERVICE ROBOTS--EVERYTHING--LOOKS DIFFERENT...
THAT WOULD BE THE INTRODUCTION OF THE STEELMEISTER'S DESIGN AND ENGINEERING...
...THE HYBRIDIZATION OF KRYPTONIAN AND EARTHLY TECHNOLOGIES.

AS YOU DESIRED, THE EARTHLY WILL NOW MODIFY AND INDOCTRINATE THE KRYPTONIAN...

...THE HOPE BEING THAT A COMBINED TECHNOLOGY WILL FURTHER CONFUSE ANY POTENTIAL DIGITAL INVADERS...

"...AS OUR RECENT EXPERIENCE WITH THE REBORN ERADICATOR PROGRAM AND THE BRAINIAC 13 VIRUS WOULD INDICATE.
"ALL TO BETTER PROTECT AND SERVE THE PLANET

"IN ADDITION TO ALL THAT, THE ESTABLISHMENT OF THIS SOLITON-ACTIVATED PORTAL TO THE PHANTOM ZONE SHOULD ALLOW YOU ACCESS, IF NECESSARY, TO THAT FAR PLANE OF EXISTENCE.

"IT'S A RISKY ENDEAVOR, NEVER BEFORE ATTEMPTED...

"...BUT WE'VE BEEN THROUGH THIS ALL BEFORE. YOU BELIEVE THE BENEFITS OUTWEIGH THE RISKS."

"AS FAR AS THE POSSIBILITY OF RECOVERING THE DIMENSIONALLY-CHALLENGED CITY OF KANDOR...
"...ALL EVIDENCE INDICATES IT SURVIVED. BUT ITS RETURN RAISES SO MANY PROBABILITY ISSUES THAT I CAN NOT BEGIN TO HAZARD...
"BIG BLUE...?"
BIG BLUE, ARE YOU, LIKE, ILL?
ARE YOU NOT FUNCTIONING AS PER YOUR NORMAL...
I--I'M OKAY-- KOFF...
...IT'S JUST-- EVERYTHING-- HAPPENING SO FAST...
...I...
WHAT'S THA...?
ALERT! ALERT!

INTRUDER ALERT!
SOMETHING HAS INVADED SYSTEMS!
BUT THEY JUST FORMED! WHAT COULD POSSIBLY...?
MAXIMUM ALERT!
AN ALIEN PRESENCE HAS INFECTED PROGRAMMING AND IS IN CONTROL OF THE PHANTOM ZONE LOCKS!
SENSORS INDICATE POLYPHEMUS 212 IS NOW IN THE PROCESS OF EXPENDING HIS FINAL ENERGIES TO THE RELEASE OF THE OTHER.
REST IN PEACE, COMRADE 212.
GENTLEMEN-- PREPARE FOR IMMEDIATE ACTION!
YOU'RE TOO LATE, SUPERMAN...
TOO LATE TO STOP ME FROM RETURNING...
...TOO LATE TO CLOSE THE DOOR ON MY VENGEANCE!

LOOK AT ME, SUPERMAN!
LOOK AT WHAT YOU'VE DONE TO ME!!
THE CYBORG!
GAKKK!
IT WORKED!
WE'RE IN!

THIS IS INSANE! WHERE DID THIS LUNATIC COME FROM...
...AND WHO ARE THOSE CHARACTERS?
WITH THE STATE OF THE FORTRESS IN FLUX, EVERYTHING MUST BE VULNERABL...
UHHHNN...
ZZRK
I SAID LOOK AT ME, SUPERMAN!!
I WANT THIS TWISTED HORROR THAT I'VE BECOME...
...TO BE THE LAST VISION THAT EVER CROSSES YOUR TREACHEROUS ALIEN EYES!
KRUNCH
SMASH
KNOCK KNOCK

UM--I JUST STOPPED BY TO-- UH--SAY HI TO NATASHA?
I COULD COME BACK IF THIS ISN'T A GOOD TIME...
BORIS!
BORIS
OUC
BRAAAPP
BRAAAPP
I'M HOME FREE, UNC!
'EM YOU STUFF
THE RANK AND FILE CYBERMOTH IS APPARENTLY NOT VERY BRIGHT--THEY DIDN'T THINK TO PUT SECURITY BACK UP!
BORIS, I WAS NEVER HAPPIER TO SEE YOU!
BRAAAPP
KKRRRRNNCH
BORIS! NATASHA! YOU KEEP YOUR HEADS DOWN!
AND YOU CREEPY VERMIN...

HEROES FACE THE ADVANCE OF
HAOS AS ONE, THEIR POWERS
ERSONIFYING THE TWO WORLDS
KNOWN TO THE ANCIENTS.
...AND THE SUN-LORD
MASTER OF THE SKY,
THE BRINGER OF LIFE
FROM THE HEAVENS.
..DON'T
OU EVER
NT A GUN
MY NIECE
GAIN!
KRAK
HE EARTH-GIANT,
E FORGE OF THE
ODS, DRAWING HIS
TRENGTH FROM THE
PLANET ITSELF...
URRRK!
NOT
IMPRESSIVE,
SUPERMAN...

...BUT, THEN AGAIN, MY TIME IN THE BLACK HORROR OF THE PHANTOM ZONE HAS MADE ME *VERY* TOUGH.

THERE ARE *HORRIBLE* THINGS THAT LIVE BETWEEN DIMENSIONS...

...THE MIND AND BODY MUST ADAPT IN *EXTRAORDINARY* WAYS TO SURVIVE.

*GASP*

HURRY! WE ONLY HAVE *MINUTES* TO SIPHON THE KRYPTONIAN COMPUTER'S ENTIRE MEMORY!

SECURITY SHIELDS MAY COME ON LINE AT ANY TIME, AND THIS BATTLE ISN'T GOING TO LAST FOREVER...

IN THE BEGINNING, THE SUN-LORD SEES HOW WEAK MANKIND IS. HE TAKES PITY AND CRUSADES TO TURN ALL MAN'S ENEMIES TO MONSTERS OF STONE.
THWACK
...I ONLY DID WHAT I HAD TO DO!
ONLY DID WHAT YOU...?
IS THAT THE BEST YOU CAN OFFER?
THIS IS ALMOST DISAPPOINTING!
WHY, LOOK AT YOU!
YOU'RE -- SICKLY...
...DISGUSTING...
BUT HE OFFENDS THE GODS ALONG THE WAY, AND MUST FACE HIS OWN DEATH...
WHAT'S HAPPENED TO YOU? I DREAMED OF TAKING YOU OUT AT THE HEIGHT OF YOUR POWER...
...BUT NOW I COULD JUST SQUASH YOU LIKE A...

...BEFORE WINNING ALLIES THAT AID IN HIS TRIUMPHANT REBIRTH.
AIEEEEE!
ZZZSSSSSSS
WHAT...
...CERIZAH-- OF KANDOR?
JUST RELAX, SUPERMAN...
SSSZZZZZZZZ
LET ME GO!
DAMN YOU! SUPERMAN IS MINE!
...WHILE THE KANDORIAN EMERGENCY SQUAD REMOVES THIS TRANSDIMENSIONAL MISTAKE!
PARALYTIC RAYS AT MAXIMUM!
IT'S OVER, CYBORG. YOU'RE GOING BACK.
HE--HE'S MINE...
KANDORIAN-- I PROMISE I WILL NOT FORGET YOUR INTERFERENCE...
CERIZAH! KOFF WE KNEW KANDOR MUST HAVE ESCAPED DESTRUCTION, BUT...
BUT WHAT ARE WE DOIN HERE?
THAT'S A FAI QUESTION...

SECONDS BEFORE E KRYPTONITE ARHEAD STRUCK OUR FORTRESS, ANDORIAN REALITY-UX SENSORS ERTED US OF THE IMPENDING DISASTER...
...OUR SCIENTISTS WERE ABLE TO CUT THE TENUOUS CORDS THAT BOUND US TO YOUR PLANE OF REALITY JUST IN TIME.

KANDOR ESCAPED DESTRUCTION, BUT WAS CAST ADRIFT...
...IN THE PHANTOM ZONE!

REMARKABLY, WE FOUND THE CYBORG THERE AS WELL! THE ZONE WOULD SEEM TO BE A SORT OF PROTOCOSMIC CATCH-ALL FOR DIMENSIONAL RIFT DEBRIS.
IRONICALLY, WE'VE BEEN ABLE TO TRACK CYBORG WITHIN THE ZONE WITH THE VERY TECHNOLOGY HE BROUGHT TO KANDOR...
...THE SAME TECHNOLOGY THAT NOW PARALYZES HIM!

BUT WE MUST HURRY BACK-- A TEMPORARY FLUX-STATE SURROUNDING THE RE-CREATION OF YOUR FORTRESS ALLOWED US THIS RARE DEPARTURE FROM KANDOR...
...BUT THAT IS DISAPPEARING AS REMATERIALIZATION APPROACHES COMPLETION.

WE MUST REJOIN KANDOR IN THE PHANTOM ZONE AND PREPARE TO AGAIN ESTABLISH OUR FRAGILE LINK WITH THE RECONSTRUCTED LABORATORY BOTTLE YOU PROVIDED.

IF ALL GOES WELL, KANDOR WILL SOON AGAIN RESIDE SAFELY WITHIN YOUR WALLS...
...UNTIL THAT DAY WHEN OUR CITY IS FREED FROM ITS TRANSDIMENSIONAL PRISON!
TILL WE MEET AGAIN, MY FRIEND... KOFF

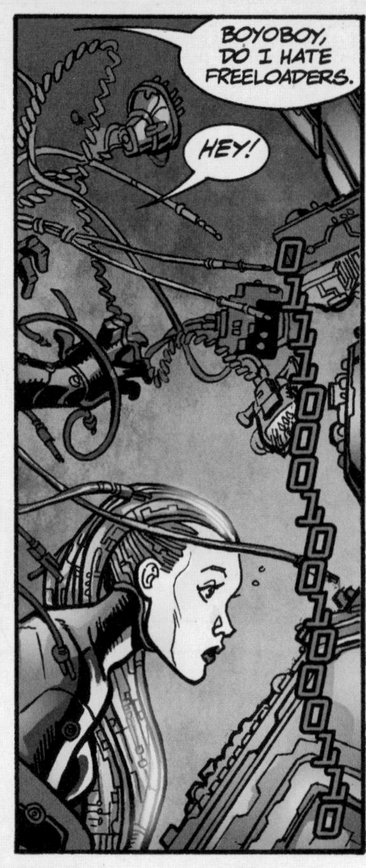
BOYOBOY, DO I HATE FREELOADERS.
HEY!

YOU!!
BUT-- BUT...

BUT YOU DIDN'T EXPECT TO SEE ME SO SOON?
SKRUUUNCH
METHINKS THE CYBORG AND YOU HAVE PLOTTED AGAINST MY HOUSE.
KONK
CURSE HIM! WE WERE SO CLOSE!
WHERE THE HELL IS THE WAY OUT...
NO...

NO! STOP!
STAY AWAY FROM THE...

WHAT'S H-HAPPENING?!
IT'S P-PULLING M-ME-- IN...
...H-HELP ME...

HELP MEEEEEE...
HOLD ON!
HOLD...

SHE'S GONE! GOT TO GO IN-- GET HER OUT...
NO, BIG BLUE, IT'S TOO LATE!
YOU CAN'T JUST FLY IN AND NAVIGATE THE PHANTOM ZONE, IT'S NOT LIKE OUR REALITY!

JUST CLOSE THE PORTAL BEFORE ITS TRANSITION FIELD DISRUPTS ANYTHING ELSE!
IF THE GIRL CAN BE RESCUED, IT WILL HAPPEN AT ANOTHER TIME.

ANOTHER TIME, THEN -- BUT I *WILL* BRING HER BACK.
WHAT'S ≶KOFF≶ OUR STATUS, KELEX?
THE ALIEN OVERRIDE HAS DISSIPATED--WE ARE AGAIN MASTERS OF OUR DOMAIN.
CONSTRUCTION IS 98.783% COMPLETE WITH NO FURTHER COMPLICATIONS ANTICIPATED. BIG...
GOOD. START *PHASE 2*--BEGIN DOWNLOADING KRYPTONIAN TECHNICAL FILES TO THE STEELWORKS... ≶KOFF≶
...I'VE GOT TO STEP OUTSIDE.

SO *MANY* OF THEM--THEY DON'T STOP...
IN THE *BEGINNING*, HE IS THE *EARTH-GIANT.* IN MORE CIVILIZED TIMES HE BECOMES THE STEEL-DRIVING FOLK HERO *JOHN HENRY*--THE HERO WHO TAKES ON THE DEHUMANIZING EXCESSES OF AN *INDUSTRIAL REVOLUTION* THAT THREATENS TO SMOTHER THE WORKING MAN.

IT'S JUST *SO* VACANT LIVING IN METROPOLIS.
YOU SHOULD *NOT* HAVE KEPT ME WAITING THIS LONG.
THROOM
THOUGHT YOU'D LEARN TO APPRECIATE ME MORE.
WOW. YOUR UNCLE IS *REALLY*-- YOU KNOW...
YEAH. HE'S GOOD AT WHAT HE DOES.
KRAK
NICE HEAVE-- *OUCH.*
THAT'S GONNA LEAVE A MARK.

OPE THE
DS GOT
UT OF
ERE.
YOU GET ENOUGH ANTS TOGETHER AND THEY'LL BRING DOWN EVEN AN ELEPHANT...
IN SPIRIT, JOHN HENRY WAS AN EARTH-GIANT. BUT IN BODY HE WAS A MAN, AND HIS SUPERHUMAN EFFORTS BROUGHT HIM AN EARLY GRAVE...

...AND THIS ELEPHANT IS WEARING...

SHOOOOM

YOU KNOW, IF YOU GUYS ARE GOING TO STICK WITH THIS INSECT THEME, YOU'RE GOING TO HEAR A LOT OF INFESTATION JOKES...
EEEP.

AND EXTERMINATOR JOKES.
AND THEN IT JUST GETS UGLY.
OKAY, PUNKS-- THE ODDS HAVE EVENED A BIT.
I'VE GOT MY SECOND WIND-- SO COME AND GET IT!
HMMM-- MAYBE THEY FEEL THE TIDE-- KOFF HAS TURNED.
AND NONE TOO SOON--MY SECOND WIND DIDN'T LAST VERY LONG.
GOOD LORD, SUPERMAN-- YOU DO NOT LOOK GOOD.
THE FORTRESS?
SAFE, SECURE, OPERATING, AND DOWNLOADING TO YOUR COMPUTERS... KOFF
WHICH MEANS I SHOULD BE ABLE TO SECURE THE 'WORKS AGAIN, THANK GOD...
UNC! BORIS AND I NEED SOMETHING TO EAT...

LOOK, I'M NOT GOING TO NAG, BUT...
...YOU ARE SEEING SOMEONE ABOUT YOUR-- CONDITION, AREN'T YOU...?
AT THE END OF THE BEGINNING, THE TWIN WAR-GODS--THE TITAN BROTHERS--THE MASTERS OF EARTH AND HEAVEN--WILL CHECK THE FORCES OF A NIHILISTIC UNIVERSE, WILL PROVIDE FOR VULNERABLE MANKIND A SAFER LANDSCAPE.
UMMM...
THIS IS THE SPOT.
SO LET'S SEE IF YOU KNOW THE COMBINATION.
BINGO ON THE FIRST TRY.
INCREDIBLE.
JUST WAIT, JOHN HENRY.
JUST WAIT.

THANK YOU, JOHN
THANK YOU FOR BRINGING ME BACK TO MY HERITAGE.
THANK YOU FOR GIVING THE WORLD ANOTHER LAYER OF PROTECTION.
LOOKS LIKE A PRETTY SOLID JOB OF CONSTRUCTION.

HEY! I JUST THOUGHT OF SOMETHING...
OH?
IF EVERYTHING REMATERIALIZED, THERE'S SOMETHING I NEED TO GIVE YOU...
WELL, I'LL BE. IT LOOKS LIKE IT IS HERE...
...IT'S NOT EXACTLY A GIFT...
...I MEAN-- *KOFF* YOU'VE CERTAINLY EARNED IT MANY TIMES OVER...
YOUR CAPE.
OUR CAPE. WE'RE PARTNERS NOW.
I MEAN, I'D BE HONORED IF...
SAY NO MORE-- PARTNER.
THANKS.
"OUR WORK--OUR LIVES--ARE NOW AS LINKED AS THE COMPUTERS BETWEEN THE FORTRESS AND THE STEELWORKS.
"WE EACH MAKE THE OTHER STRONGER."
NOW--I NEED TO TALK WITH YOU ABOUT THE INFLUENCE YOUR NIECE IS HAVING ON MY ROBOT...
TOGETHER, THEY HOLD BACK CHAOS LITTLE BIT LONGER.

SECRETS OF THE
JOR-EL AND LARA.
Thirty-foot statues created by Superman in honor of his birth parents watch over the entrance to various living quarters.
2
1
SUNSTONE SIMULATOR.
Created out of the sunstone memory crystals sent with Superman to Earth, this databank holds the historical and scientific knowledge of Krypton. Hosted by a simulation of his father, Jor-El, this extra-terrestrial computer is Superman's most valuable and cherished heirloom.
3
INTERPLANETARY HABITAT.
Across the universe, Superman has rescued an array of extraterrestrial animals on the verge of extinction including the Thought-Beast, the Duplorian Hawk, the Metal Boar and the Black Mercy.

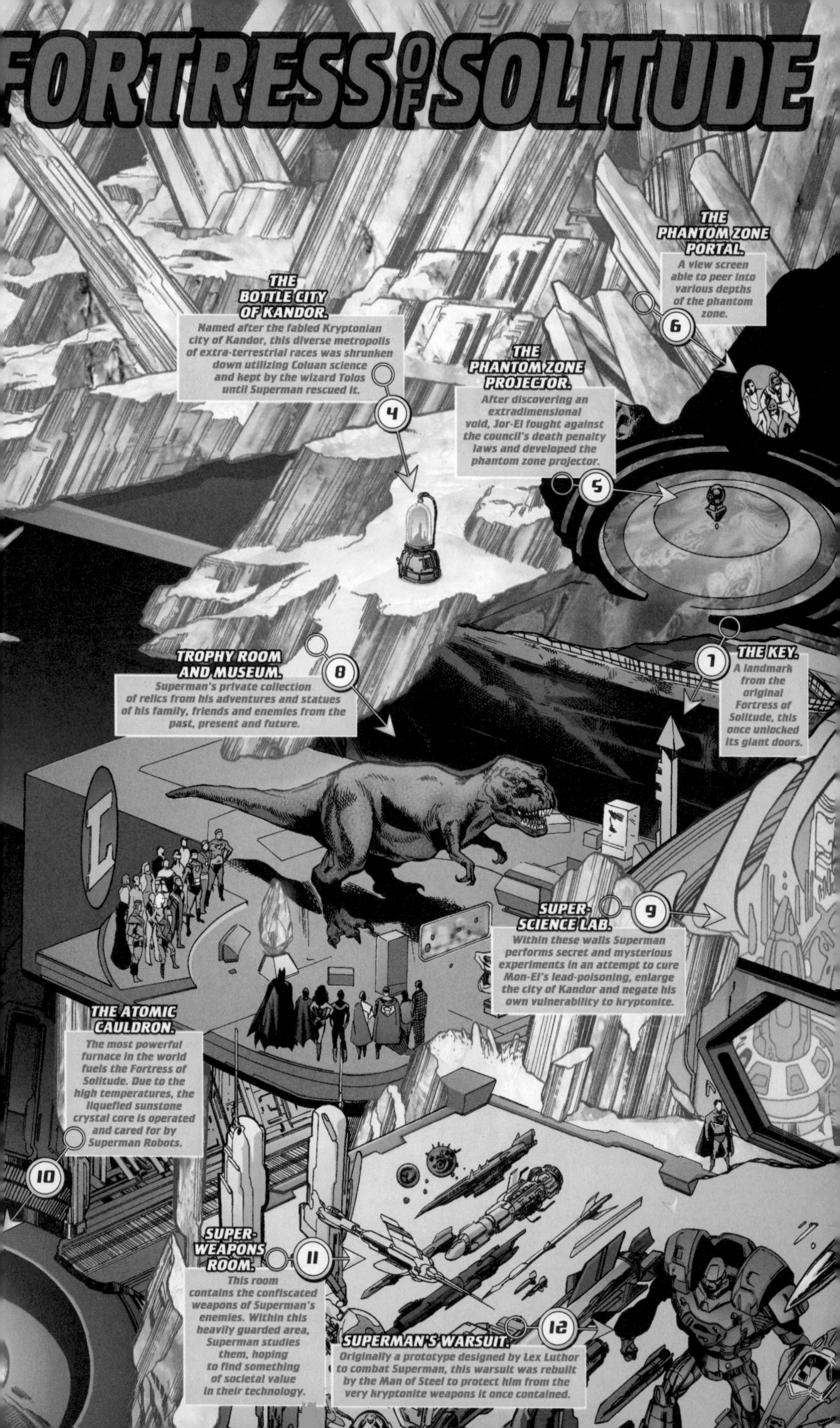
FORTRESS OF SOLITUDE
THE BOTTLE CITY OF KANDOR.
Named after the fabled Kryptonian city of Kandor, this diverse metropolis of extra-terrestrial races was shrunken down utilizing Coluan science and kept by the wizard Tolos until Superman rescued it.
4
THE PHANTOM ZONE PORTAL.
A view screen able to peer into various depths of the phantom zone.
6
THE PHANTOM ZONE PROJECTOR.
After discovering an extradimensional void, Jor-El fought against the council's death penalty laws and developed the phantom zone projector.
5
TROPHY ROOM AND MUSEUM.
Superman's private collection of relics from his adventures and statues of his family, friends and enemies from the past, present and future.
8
7
THE KEY.
A landmark from the original Fortress of Solitude, this once unlocked its giant doors.
SUPER-SCIENCE LAB.
Within these walls Superman performs secret and mysterious experiments in an attempt to cure Mon-El's lead-poisoning, enlarge the city of Kandor and negate his own vulnerability to kryptonite.
9
THE ATOMIC CAULDRON.
The most powerful furnace in the world fuels the Fortress of Solitude. Due to the high temperatures, the liquefied sunstone crystal core is operated and cared for by Superman Robots.
10
SUPER-WEAPONS ROOM.
This room contains the confiscated weapons of Superman's enemies. Within this heavily guarded area, Superman studies them, hoping to find something of societal value in their technology.
11
SUPERMAN'S WARSUIT.
Originally a prototype designed by Lex Luthor to combat Superman, this warsuit was rebuilt by the Man of Steel to protect him from the very kryptonite weapons it once contained.
12